THE ARTISANAL KITCHEN

BARBECUE RULES

THE ARTISANAL KITCHEN

BARBECUE RULES

LESSONS & RECIPES FOR SUPERIOR SMOKING & GRILLING

JOE CARROLL & NICK FAUCHALD

Photographs by William Hereford

Artisan | New York

CONTENTS

ON THE SIDE 91

INTRODUCTION

This book is a straightforward approach to smoking and grilling, with key lessons and, of course, mouthwatering recipes to help you apply what you've learned. Live-fire cooking is pretty simple, but it relies on a real understanding of how smoke, fire, and ingredients interact, as well as on conscientious and informed shopping.

Amazing food can be cooked on almost any kind of equipment if you know how to build and maintain a fire, are able to get high-quality ingredients, and can master time and temperature. This book will teach you the importance of wood as fuel and the many shapes and forms it can take. And it will show you how great meals begin at the butcher shop and farmers' market.

Finally, one of best things about live-fire cooking is the sense of celebration that comes with it. With this book, you can create a range of smoky and grilled meats that will satisfy any palate, as well as side dishes to round out the table. My hope is that whether you want to smoke a better brisket or experiment with some uncommon barbecue (pulled goat leg, perhaps?), you'll absorb these live-fire lessons and recipes and then adapt them to your own style. Happy cooking!

SMOKED

Meat + smoke + patience = barbecue. You need only these three things to make the best slow-smoked meat you've ever tasted. Barbecue is a relatively simple process once you know where to focus your attention.

Choosing the best meat is by far the most important step in achieving barbecue greatness (see page 23), yet wood should be treated like an ingredient too (see page 40). Once you learn to select the right meat and wood for whatever you're smoking, you're ready to choose your equipment. The style of smoker you use will automatically inform your choice of primary fuel: gas, charcoal, or hardwood logs. In this chapter, I take you through your options and, I hope, convince you that less is more, both in price and complexity of equipment.

Once you have your smoker, I'll show you how to set it up for barbecuing, and how to monitor and maintain your 'cue throughout the low-and-slow process. After that, you're ready to choose your first barbecue adventure from the recipes that begin on page 19.

CHOOSING A SMOKER

I taught myself how to barbecue in my backyard with a $40 Brinkmann smoker, which continues to turn out some of the best meat I've ever smoked. You can spend hundreds or even thousands of dollars on a fancy high-end smoker, but all you're paying for is convenience and, perhaps, some badass-looking equipment—but certainly not flavor.

ELECTRIC SMOKERS

An electric smoker is the easiest to use: you plug it in, set the temperature, load your meat, and let the machine do its work; all you have to do is add some wood chips periodically. What you'll end up with is, yes, technically, barbecue, but it's almost impossible to create a thick, flavorful bark in an electric smoker, and you can forget about a smoke ring (see page 47). Simply put, electric smokers don't produce the combustion needed to create the flavor of authentic barbecue.

PROPANE SMOKERS

Propane smokers are as easy to use as electric smokers but are much more portable. As with a gas grill, there's no charcoal fire to attend to, and you can achieve something close to barbecue flavor. But, as with gas grills, something very important is missing: wood.

PELLET SMOKERS

Like electric and gas smokers, pellet smokers offer accurate temperature control and require only minimal babysitting during the smoking process. These grill-like rigs burn small cylinders of compressed sawdust to produce a constant output of smoke. While pellet smokers have their fans and are great for cold-smoking, I've found them to produce less smoke—and therefore less flavor—than even electric and gas smokers.

CHARCOAL SMOKERS

Consistent temperature is a convenience, but what's lacking in all of the models mentioned above is charcoal. While fresh wood, whether in the form of chips, pellets, or chunks, adds flavor, carbonized wood— that is, charcoal—is equally essential to achieving maximum barbecue flavor.

Most charcoal smokers fall into one of two categories: offset or bullet-shaped. Offset smokers look like a grill with a small firebox attached to one side. The heat and smoke produced in the firebox flow through the barrel-shaped chamber and out through a chimney. It's easier to build and maintain a fire in this style of smoker, but I've found that they're very inconsistent. It's hard to control the flow of smoke, which tends to float above the meat and exit the chimney before it's done its job. Plus, the side of the chamber near the firebox gets much hotter than the opposite side, so the meat will cook unevenly unless you move it around.

My favorite type of smoker is the bullet-shaped barrel smoker. Most models resemble a kettle grill with a long metal tube fixed between the bowl-shaped bottom and the domed lid. The setup for all of these smokers is basically the same: Charcoal and wood go in a pan on the bottom of the grill and then are added through a small door as needed. A water pan is set above the charcoal and below two or more racks to hold the meat. On top goes the lid, which usually has air vents and a thermometer. The most popular barrel smoker on the market is probably the Weber Smokey Mountain (see Resources, page 108), which comes in three sizes. The cheaper Brinkmann smoker is similar in form and function, but it lacks the Weber's adjustable air vents and has a smaller door, which makes adding charcoal and wood more of a pain. It also has a rather vague temperature gauge on the lid (with "low," "medium," and "hot" zones) in lieu of an actual thermometer. (With any smoker, I recommend using an accurate oven thermometer or instant-read probe thermometer to monitor the temperature until you calibrate the built-in thermometer to your desired cooking range.)

But you don't actually need a dedicated smoker to make proper barbecue. A kettle grill can easily be configured into a smoker and will achieve equally great results once you know how to set one up (see page 15).

My advice: If you're new to barbecue, start with an inexpensive bullet smoker (see Resources, page 108). If you catch the barbecue bug after using it for a while, upgrade to something that suits your particular needs (capacity, speed, convenience, etc.). Just remember that if you opt for convenience over charcoal, you're also leaving out flavor.

SETTING UP AND USING A CHARCOAL SMOKER

If you have a charcoal smoker, congratulations! Your barbecue is going to taste great. Now it's time to start smoking. (See page 17 for step-by-step photos.)

1 Remove any ash and debris if the smoker has been previously used and clean the grates.

2 Fill a chimney starter about halfway with hardwood charcoal. Loosely crumple a couple of pieces of newspaper and drizzle or spray them with vegetable oil (this helps the paper burn longer and speeds up the charcoal-lighting process). Stuff the paper into the chimney's lower chamber, place the chimney on the smoker's top grate, and light it. Let the charcoal burn until the coals are glowing red and coated in gray ash, about 15 minutes. Put on a pair of heavy-duty fireproof gloves and carefully dump about half of the smoldering charcoal into the charcoal container. I like to keep a kettle grill or an extra chimney starter nearby and keep a steady supply of burning charcoal in it to replenish the fire—if you're using pure hardwood charcoal, you can throw a couple of unlit chunks into the smoker at a time, but charcoal briquettes must be lighted beforehand or they'll add nasty flavors to the meat.

3 Line the water pan with aluminum foil (this makes cleanup easier), position it over the coals, and fill it about half full with hot water. The water pan's primary function is to catch the fat that drips from the meat to prevent flare-ups, but it also acts as insulation that helps reduce temperature fluctuations.

4 Set the metal grates in place, adding the meat to the grates. If you're not filling up the entire smoker with meat, load it from the top down, as there will be a higher concentration of smoke near the top of the unit. Then put the lid on top.

5 If your smoker has air vents in the top or bottom, open them up all the way. You can adjust the vents later to control the temperature.

6 Open the smoker door and throw a few tennis ball–size chunks of wood or a handful of wood chips on top of the charcoal. Wood chips should always be soaked in water for at least 15 minutes and drained before use, but there's no need to soak wood chunks in water. If you're using chips, keep a ready supply of them soaking nearby.

7 If you have a probe thermometer, insert it through the top air vent to monitor the temperature. The smoker will take about 10 minutes to reach 225°F, which is the optimal temperature for cooking most barbecue. As you get accustomed to your smoker, you'll find yourself needing to check the thermometer less and less.

8 You'll notice that the temperature will fluctuate up and down as the wood chunks or chips ignite and the charcoal burns down. These fluctuations are inevitable with a charcoal smoker and are nothing to worry about. Your goal is to maintain a range between 200° and 250°F: As the temperature nears 200°F, add a couple of pieces of charcoal (keep a pair of long tongs handy for opening the hot door and adding the charcoal and wood). If the temperature spikes above 250°F for more than a few minutes, remove a piece or two of charcoal or partially close the bottom vent (and top vent, if necessary) to lower the temperature. If your smoker doesn't have air vents, you can briefly remove the lid until the smoker cools down, though this lets a lot of smoke escape.

⑨ When you notice the supply of smoke dying down, add one or two more wood chunks or another handful of chips to the charcoal container. When the meat nears doneness, I stop adding wood to the fire—any smoke created in the final cooking stage adds little to the overall flavor (see How Often to Add Wood, page 20).

⑩ If you're smoking big cuts of meat, the barbecue process can take all day. While it's impossible to "set it and forget it" with a charcoal smoker, you don't need to constantly babysit your barbecue. Check the temperature and smoke level every hour or so, and add small amounts of charcoal and wood as needed. As long as your mean temperature is around 225°F, you'll have nothing to worry about.

BARBECUE TIMES AND TEMPERATURES

The following chart gives smoking times and temperatures for the various meats and cuts most commonly used for barbecue. The target smoking temperature for most barbecue is 225°F.

You'll notice that the range of cooking times for any given meat can be quite large; this is because of many small factors, including the temperature of the meat when it begins cooking, the mean temperature of your smoker, the temperature *outside* of your smoker, and even the breed of animal. I've included a target internal temperature for when the meat is done, but that is far less important than the texture of the meat, which you should check first, following the recipe's directions.

MEAT	APPROXIMATE WEIGHT/SIZE	IDEAL SMOKER TEMPERATURE	APPROXIMATE COOKING TIME	INTERNAL TEMPERATURE WHEN DONE
Beef brisket (whole)	10 to 14 pounds	225°F	12 to 16 hours	185° to 195°F
Beef short ribs	7 pounds per rack	225°F	5 to 6 hours	180°F
Beef tongue	2 to 3 pounds each	225°F	6 to 8 hours	175°F
Beef cheeks	1 pound each	225°F	5 to 7 hours	175°F
Pork shoulder (Boston butt)	5 to 8 pounds	225°F	7 to 13 hours (1½ hours per pound)	185° to 195°F
Pork spareribs	3 pounds per rack	225°F	5 to 7 hours	180°F
Pork belly	12 to 15 pounds	225°F	7 to 9 hours	175°F
Pork baby back ribs	1½ pounds per rack	225°F	3 to 5 hours	180°F
Pork loin roast	5 to 6 pounds	300°F	2 to 4 hours	140°F
Fresh sausages	1½ to 2 inches in diameter	225°F	1 to 2 hours	165°F
Lamb shoulder	8 to 10 pounds	225°F	4 to 6 hours	185°F
Lamb spareribs	1½ pounds per rack	225°F	3 to 5 hours	150°F
Goat leg	5 pounds	225°F	5 to 8 hours	150°F
Chicken	4 pounds	225°F	3 to 5 hours	165°F
Turkey	12 to 14 pounds	225°F	6 to 7 hours	165°F

SMOKING IN A KETTLE GRILL

Kettle grills make pretty good smokers. The main disadvantage is that you have to open the cover to add more charcoal and wood or to check your meat, which lets out heat and precious smoke. So, to make sure you do that as infrequently as possible, use hardwood chunks over wood chips; they take longer to burn down and, thus, will release smoke over a longer time. Otherwise, the process is very similar to using a dedicated smoker.

1 Remove any ash and debris if the smoker has been previously used and clean the grates.

2 Prepare a chimney starter according to the instructions in step 2 on page 13, filling it about halfway with coals. Dump the charcoal into one side of the grill—over the bottom air vent if your grill has one—leaving the other half free of coals. Place a disposable aluminum tray on the other side to use as a drip pan.

❺ Place a few hardwood chunks or a foil packet of wood chips (see page 18) over the coals. Add the top grate and put your meat over the drip pan. Cover the grill, placing the air vents in the lid over the meat. Open both vents about halfway.

❻ Smoke the meat, monitoring the smoker temperature on a thermometer inserted through the top vent. If the grill gets too hot, close the top vent and, if necessary, partly close the bottom vent. If using hardwood chunks, add a couple of pieces of unlit hardwood charcoal when the temperature dips down near 200°F. Or, if your wood chip packet stops producing smoke, remove it with tongs and replace it with a fresh packet. If the wood chips ignite, douse the flames with a squirt bottle.

SMOKING IN A GAS GRILL

Gas grills have the advantage of easy temperature control, but you're going to miss out on charcoal flavor. And gas grills tend to be poorly ventilated, which allows a lot of smoke to escape rather than circulate around the meat. Most gas grills have at least two burners; if yours has only one, you won't be able to smoke on it—sorry.

❶ If your grill lights from left to right, turn one burner to medium and put the meat on the opposite side of the grill (you don't have to wait for the grill to heat up; and there's no need for a drip pan with a gas setup unless you want to make cleanup easier). Put a wood chip packet (see page 18) under the grate over the lit flame. If your grill lights front to back, light the front burner, place the wood chip packet under the grate over the burner, and put the meat as far back on the grill as possible.

❷ Smoke the meat, adjusting the burner to maintain your desired temperature. Replace the wood chip packet whenever it stops smoking; each packet should last for 30 to 45 minutes.

SETTING UP A CHARCOAL SMOKER

① Fill a chimney starter halfway with charcoal. Light the charcoal and let it burn until the coals are coated with ash.

② Fill the water pan halfway with warm water.

③ Throw in a few chunks of wood.

④ Set the metal grates in place and add the meat, loading the smoker from the top down.

WOOD CHIP PACKETS

Whenever you're smoking on a grill (charcoal or gas) or when you want to add an extra hit of smoke to whatever you're grilling, throw a foil packet of wood chips onto the coals, or under the grate and over the burner on a gas grill. To make one, pile a couple of handfuls of soaked wood chips on a square of aluminum foil. Top with another square of foil and fold the sides up to form a packet. Cut several slits in the top of the packet with a paring knife to allow the smoke to escape. Prepare several of these before you light the grill. Each one should last for 30 to 45 minutes before it needs to be replaced, and you can always freeze any extra packets until you're ready to use them; they'll work straight out of the freezer.

PULLED PORK SHOULDER

Pulled pork is a good way to introduce yourself to low-and-slow smoking. Pork shoulder is a far more forgiving cut than brisket; it's well marbled and has plenty of intramuscular fat, as well as a nice fatty layer underneath the skin. It's also not as sensitive to changes in temperature: if your smoker runs hot, you won't risk drying out the pork. The hardest part of making pulled pork is waiting to tear into it.

SHOULDER

MAKES 10 TO 12 SERVINGS

ONE 8-POUND BONE-IN BOSTON BUTT (AKA PORK SHOULDER ROAST)

1 CUP FETTE SAU DRY RUB (PAGE 22), PLUS (OPTIONAL) MORE FOR SEASONING

KOSHER SALT (OPTIONAL)

POTATO ROLLS OR HAMBURGER BUNS, FOR SERVING

WOOD CHUNKS OR SOAKED WOOD CHIPS

❶ Put the pork shoulder on a rimmed baking sheet and cover it generously with the dry rub, making sure to stuff and pat the rub into any cracks and crevices in the meat. If you have time, let the pork rest for 1 hour at room temperature, or until the rub starts to turn into a pasty coating.

❷ Preheat a smoker to 225°F or set up a grill for smoking (see page 13 or 16).

❸ Put the pork in the smoker and smoke, maintaining a smoker temperature of between 225° and 250°F, replenishing the charcoal and wood chunks or chips as needed.

❹ After about 8 hours, begin checking the pork periodically. When it is done, you should be able to easily pull a hunk of meat off with your fingers; the pork should have a thick, chewy bark and a noticeable pink smoke ring (see The Smoke Ring, page 47) just below the surface. With a towel or thick rubber gloves, grab the bone and give it a wiggle; if it's loose enough to pull from the shoulder, the pork is ready; an instant-read thermometer inserted into the center of the meat should register between 185° and 195°F. Total smoking time can be up to 13 hours.

⑤ Using heavy rubber gloves, transfer the pork to a rimmed baking sheet. Let it rest for at least 30 minutes.

⑥ Remove the bone, if you haven't already, and begin pulling the pork into pieces. I find it speeds up the process if you first smash the shoulder a few times with the base of your palm; this will separate it into a few larger pieces, which you can grab and pick apart. As you pull the pork, discard any large pieces of fat that you come across.

⑦ Once all of the pork is pulled to your liking, taste a piece and, if necessary, season the meat with salt or dry rub. Serve with potato rolls or hamburger buns and sauce on the side, if you like. The pork can be made up to 1 day ahead.

NOTE

To rewarm the pork, put it in a roasting pan or casserole, add a splash of barbecue sauce, vinegar, or water, and cover with a lid or foil. Rewarm in a 250°F oven.

HOW OFTEN TO ADD WOOD

As with any other seasoning, it's possible to use too little or too much wood smoke on your barbecue. I prefer to use more smoke earlier on, keeping a constant supply circulating around the meat for approximately the first half of the cooking time, and then adding wood less frequently or backing off completely toward the end. I do this for two reasons: Meat absorbs smoke more easily at lower temperatures and by smoking it early in the process, I can guarantee that it will have ample wood-smoke flavor. And if you add too much smoke toward the end of cooking, the meat can take on an acrid flavor.

FETTE SAU DRY RUB

This rub can be used on any meat. Feel free to improvise on the ingredients and amounts, reducing the sugar for a less-sweet bark (crust), increasing the cayenne for a spicier one, and so on.

MAKES ABOUT 4 CUPS

1½ CUPS PACKED DARK BROWN SUGAR

1 CUP KOSHER SALT

1 CUP GROUND ESPRESSO BEANS

¼ CUP FRESHLY GROUND BLACK PEPPER

¼ CUP GARLIC POWDER

2 TABLESPOONS GROUND CINNAMON

2 TABLESPOONS GROUND CUMIN

2 TABLESPOONS CAYENNE PEPPER

Combine the sugar, salt, espresso beans, black pepper, garlic powder, cinnamon, cumin, and cayenne in a resealable container, cover tightly, and shake well to combine. Store in a cool, dry place. The rub will keep for up to 2 months, at which point the coffee will begin to taste stale.

MEAT MATTERS

No matter how good your equipment, technique, or fuel, you will never achieve barbecue nirvana or a perfectly grilled steak if you don't start with high-quality ingredients, such as heritage breeds and locally raised animals.

What's more, it's easy to make a case against eating meat from factory-farmed animals. You're eating animals bred to grow as quickly as possible (and often to be leaner and less flavorful); these are animals that have been raised on chemically treated feed in dirty, inhumane conditions. And you're eating animals raised with methods that hurt the environment in countless ways. So buying high-quality sustainably raised meat is not just about choosing meat that's far more delicious; it's about not putting crap into your body and not contributing to an industry that is hurting us and the planet.

My simple style of barbecue won't give you the best results if you don't use the best meat you can get your hands on. No matter how perfectly you smoke or grill a piece of protein—or how you dress it up with rubs, sauces, and accompaniments—if you start with a mediocre product, you'll end up with one. On the other hand, a flavorful cut needs very little to become the best piece of meat you've ever tasted.

In order to get the best meat available, you have to ask some questions: Where did the meat come from? How were the animals raised? What were they fed? When and how was the meat processed, packed, stored, and shipped? To help you answer these, consider the following criteria—listed in descending order of importance—when buying meat.

❶ NATURALLY RAISED

First and foremost, the meat you cook and eat should be from animals raised without the use of antibiotics, hormones, steroids, or other growth-promoting medicines or chemicals. They should also have been fed an additive-free, 100-percent vegetarian diet. Unfortunately, the USDA's formal definition of "natural" requires only that the meat has been minimally processed, with no preservatives or artificial ingredients added. And that is true of pretty much all fresh meat, rendering the "natural" label meaningless. It leaves room for animals that have been treated with hormones and antibiotics at some point in their lives. So the label alone probably won't tell you if you're buying my definition of "naturally raised" meat; you need to ask your butcher or farmer or do a little research to determine its provenance.

❷ HERITAGE BREED

Whenever possible, buy meat from heritage breeds. These animals thrive in open pastures and are more resistant to disease and parasites, making antibiotics less necessary. Plus the meat from heritage animals always tastes better than that of their commercial counterparts, as they've been bred for flavor, not productivity. Of course, raising these breeds requires more time, effort, and money than an industrial operation, and the costs are carried over to the customer. But the extra expense is worth it.

❸ SMALL FARM–RAISED

There will be large farming operations whose animals meet the previous two criteria, but if you have the option, buy from smaller, family-run farms. First, it's good to support their business: small farms are an ecological asset that promotes biodiversity and sustainable agricultural practices. I've also found that small-scale farmers treat their animals with an extra degree of care: if nothing else, each animal in a small operation is that much more essential to the bottom line. Generally speaking, the closer you can get to the source of the meat, the easier it is to know that you're buying a great product.

❹ LOCALLY RAISED

You should always favor quality over proximity, but when you can find great meat raised close to home, on local farms, buy it. If you can't find high-quality options anywhere close to where you live, there are many online retailers that specialize in heritage and responsibly raised animals (see Resources, page 108, for some of my favorites).

⑤ ORGANIC

In order for its meat to be labeled "organic" by the USDA, a farm must comply with a strict set of requirements: its animals must be born and raised on certified organic pastures with unrestricted outdoor access, must never receive hormones or antibiotics, and must subsist on a certified organic diet. But getting certified as an organic farm is a time-consuming and expensive process that many smaller operations can't afford—although they can't label their food as such, many of these farms do follow organic practices. So if the meat you buy satisfies all of the other criteria *and* is really organic, consider it a bonus.

HOW TO IDENTIFY GOOD MEAT

It would be wonderful if we could always know the history of every piece of meat we purchase, but reality often leaves us staring into a butcher case or meat aisle full of anonymous protein without a clue about what to choose. To help you make the right choice in those situations, follow this animal-by-animal guide.

BEEF

Much of beef's overall quality is determined by breed, how the cow was raised, what it was fed, and when and how it was processed. But fat content is another indication of quality, and it's the easiest to spot with your own two eyes when nothing else of the beef's provenance is known. More marbling—that is, thin striations of intramuscular fat— equals more flavor and tenderness. The USDA helps determine how much marbling is present in a cut of beef by assigning it one of eight grading levels.

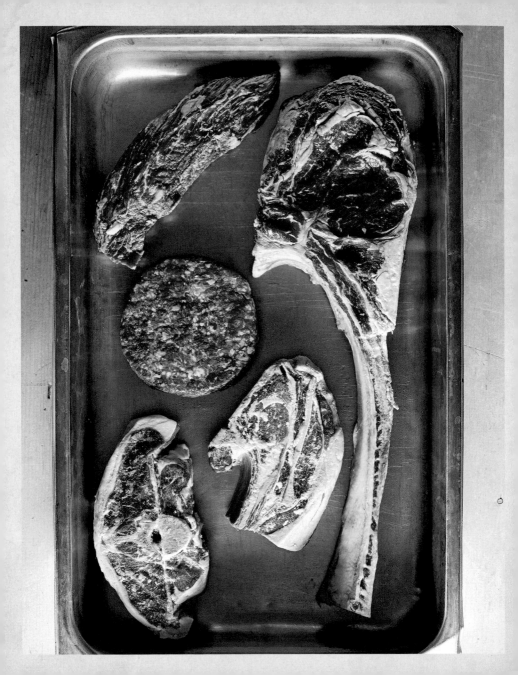

The USDA grades you need to know about for the purpose of barbecue and grilling are the three top grades: prime, choice, and select. Select meat contains a slight amount of marbling, and it's what you'll probably encounter at the supermarket. But its low fat content means that select beef is best suited to braising and other wet-cooking methods. Choice beef, which you'll encounter most often at restaurants and butcher shops, has more marbling (about twice as much as select) and is a good option for most grilling and barbecue applications. Prime beef is the best of the beast; it has the most intramuscular fat and, thus, will be the most tender and flavorful.

Keep in mind that not all beef in the United States is graded; while all beef must pass USDA inspection, grading is strictly optional. You should also know that any adjectives not preceded by "USDA" that are used to describe beef—"premium," "butcher's choice," "prime selection," and so on—are meaningless marketing terms and should be ignored.

You've probably come across the term "Certified Angus Beef" on menus and in the butcher case. This trademarked brand name means that the beef has met a specific set of criteria and is either prime or (much more likely) choice. It does not mean, however, that the meat came from a pure-breed Angus steer. The Angus breed is prized among producers for its marbling and speed of maturation and, as such, is often used for crossbreeding. The defining characteristic USDA inspectors look for is a hide that's at least 51 percent black, which indicates that there are *some* Angus genes in the animal, but they do not conduct genetic testing to verify the exact makeup.

You still have more choices to make when buying beef. While marbling accounts for much of a cut's flavor and tenderness, how (and if) the meat was aged also has an effect. Once it's processed and the muscles have relaxed from rigor mortis, beef can be packaged and sold as "fresh" or further matured through either wet- or dry-aging. "Wet-aged" beef has been vacuum-packed and allowed to mature in a refrigerated environment; it is considered wet-aged because it is in contact with its own blood in its airtight packaging. Most supermarket meat has been wet-aged to some degree. The process will tenderize the meat slightly, but it doesn't have a profound effect on the flavor.

"Dry-aged" beef has been allowed to hang out in contact with the air under tightly controlled conditions for several weeks or longer, which gives enzymes, microbes, and oxygen time to react with the meat and fat. This process changes the flavor of the meat; the longer it's aged, the more concentrated its beefy flavor becomes. Beef that's been dry-aged for an extended period of time will take on a gamey, fermented—some say cheesy or mushroom-like—flavor. During dry-aging, beef can lose up to one-third of its weight through moisture loss, but what it loses in water, it gains in flavor (and, ultimately, price). Dry-aged beef is usually available only at butcher shops or the fanciest of supermarkets.

Most of the high-quality meat in America comes from animals pasture-raised on grass, then fattened on a grain-based diet in feedlots before processing. There's no denying that the meat from "grain-finished" cattle is fattier than that from cows that eat only grass until slaughter. 100-percent grass-fed beef is leaner and, thus, less tender when cooked—especially on the grill or with other high-heat methods. Grass-fed beef is plenty flavorful, though in a different way from grain-finished beef. Some people say it's gamey or fishy-tasting; others love the flavor.

Note that I haven't said anything about color when it comes to choosing beef. Modern processing and packaging technology makes it easy for producers to preserve the rosy-red color of fresh meat well beyond its sell-by date. A piece of beef that isn't cherry red isn't something to be afraid of, as long as you're buying it from a source that can tell you enough about the meat to determine its quality.

If you can't find out where your meat came from, how it was raised, or how the USDA has graded its quality, you have to rely on your eyes. Is the meat well streaked with little veins of fat, or is it mostly muscle? If the latter, skip it when grilling or barbecuing and seek out another piece. When all else fails, find a butcher and start asking questions.

PORK

Always choose heritage-breed pork. Not only is heritage-breed pork fattier and more flavorful than commercial pork, but it's better for you and the environment as well.

Berkshire, Duroc, Tamworth, Red Wattle, Large Black, Ossabaw, and Mangalitsa are some of the best breeds available, and each of these breeds varies somewhat in texture, fattiness, and flavor. The specific breed doesn't matter all that much: if you're choosing naturally raised noncommercial pork, you're probably going to end up with something great. Note: The USDA doesn't use multiple grading tiers for pork. The only two grades are "Acceptable" and "Utility," and fresh meat in the latter category can't be sold to consumers.

An animal's diet always has an effect on its flavor, but this is especially true of pork. Farmers who care about their pigs will provide them with a diverse diet that combines organic grain-based feed with whatever the pigs can forage and root up in the fields and forests where they're raised. If you're buying pork directly from a farmer, he will be able to tell you about its diet, as will any good butcher.

Commercial pork is pale pink at best, while heritage-breed meat ranges from dark pink to dark red. When selecting pork, keep in mind that you want it to look more like the color of beef than that of chicken. Lastly, look at the fat content. This will vary based on the breed and cut, but you want noticeable intramuscular marbling and a smooth, white fat cap.

LAMB

Good news: lamb is even easier to buy than pork or beef. Americans eat far less lamb than other meat, so there's a much smaller commercial market and none of the health and environmental hazards that come along with large-scale production. Most of us will find at most two or three lamb options at the market or butcher shop: American, New Zealand, and (less often) Australian. Pricewise, American lamb is the most expensive.

Like domestic beef, American lamb is usually grain-finished, which increases marbling and gives it a sweeter, mellower flavor than its southern-hemisphere counterparts. Most of America's large lamb producers are based in Colorado or the Midwest, though you can find small farms that specialize in lamb in many parts of the country, allowing you to buy locally raised meat.

CHICKEN

Because chickens are one of the easiest animals to raise in a natural environment without drugs, chemically enhanced feed, and so on, "good" chicken is more accessible than any other type of protein at the supermarket. But the bad news is that chicken is tagged with a lot of confusing labels. Knowing what these terms mean (or don't mean) will help you choose the right bird.

NATURAL

As with other meats, "natural" can be a misleading term. It only means that, upon slaughter, no artificial ingredients (flavoring, coloring, etc.) were added, so the word doesn't have anything to do with quality. Most of what you'll find at the supermarket counts as natural chicken.

HORMONE-FREE AND RAISED WITHOUT ANTIBIOTICS

Even industrially raised chickens cannot be given hormones, so "hormone-free" is just an empty marketing phrase. "Raised without antibiotics" has slightly more weight—it means that the bird (including in its egg form) was never treated with antibiotics. But there's currently no inspection process to verify this claim, and it also doesn't restrict the use of nonantibiotic medicines and chemicals. Even chickens that have been pumped full of antibiotics are technically "antibiotic-free" (though the term is not allowed on labels) at the time of slaughter, because of a required withdrawal period.

CAGE-FREE

No commercial chicken ever sees the inside of a cage: a bird that lives its entire life in a giant commercial coop is technically "cage-free," so you should ignore this label too.

FREE-RANGE

"Free-range" is another ambiguous term. By law, free-range chickens must be given access to the outdoors, but access in this case may be nothing more than a small door to a fenced-in concrete yard that the chickens never venture into from their giant factory-farm coop. Again, it's a term best ignored.

PASTURED

"Pastured" chickens are free to forage for grass, seeds, or insects. Thanks to their diverse diet, pastured chickens are usually expensive but flavorful.

ORGANIC

The USDA has created strict guidelines for birds labeled "organic." In this context, the term means that the bird's feed has also been certified organic—that is, the grain it eats has been grown in a chemical- and GMO-free field.

KOSHER AND HALAL

These chickens have been slaughtered by hand according to strict religious guidelines. Anyone concerned with how chickens are slaughtered might seek these out. Kosher chickens are also usually treated with salt, which has a similar effect to brining.

AIR-CHILLED

Most chickens are chilled in pools of cold chlorinated water after slaughter. Air-chilled chickens are hung individually in a cold environment. This reduces the risk of contamination, and it also affects the bird's texture and flavor. Air-chilled chickens aren't plumped with added water, which would dilute their flavor. Air-chilling also results in crisper skin.

HERITAGE-BREED

Heritage-breed chickens are not common, so snatch these up if you see them at your farmers' market or a specialty meat shop. If you can't find a heritage bird, look for an organic one that was air-chilled. Steer clear of any chickens with huge breasts; this is an indicator of a commercial breed favored for output, not flavor, and bad farming practices are sure to be involved.

PORK BELLY

You've likely eaten loads of smoked pork belly—it's called bacon. But this pork belly is like nothing you've ever tasted. The meat is super-moist and pillowy, and the fat is so soft it actually melts in your mouth.

BELLY

MAKES 10 TO 12 SERVINGS

1 PORK BELLY (12 TO 15 POUNDS), SKIN REMOVED

1 CUP FETTE SAU DRY RUB (PAGE 22)

WOOD CHUNKS OR SOAKED WOOD CHIPS

NOTE

Barbecue pork belly is best eaten as soon as possible, but if you have to cook it ahead of time, let it cool to room temperature, then wrap it in multiple layers of plastic and refrigerate. To rewarm the belly, unwrap it and place it in a roasting pan. Add a splash of water and cover with foil, then heat it in a 200°F oven until warmed through. If the bark has gone soft, you can recrisp it over a medium-hot grill fire for a few minutes.

❶ Put the belly on a rimmed baking sheet and coat with the dry rub, patting it onto the surface until the meat has an even layer of rub. Let the pork rest for 1 to 2 hours at room temperature, or until the rub starts to turn into a pasty coating.

❷ Preheat a smoker to 225°F or set up a grill for smoking (see page 13 or 16).

❸ Place the belly, fatty side up, in the smoker and smoke, maintaining a smoker temperature of between 210° and 225°F, replenishing the charcoal and wood chunks or chips as needed.

❹ After about 6 hours, start checking the meat periodically: Poke the belly in a few places; the fat should be gelatinous and custard-like in consistency, and the meat will easily separate under your finger. If you think the belly is nearly finished, cut off a chunk and eat it. The bark should be dry and crisp, and the meat should be moist and very tender but not mushy. An instant-read thermometer inserted into the center of the belly should register around 175°F. Total smoking time can be up to 9 hours.

❺ When the belly is smoked to your liking, use two pairs of tongs or a pair of heavy rubber gloves to transfer it to a cutting board. Let the meat rest for at least 15 minutes, then cut the belly crosswise into 1/4-inch slices and serve.

ST. LOUIS-STYLE PORK SPARERIBS

Pork spareribs are meaty and moist, with a deep, porky flavor and just enough marbling to keep them moist.

Many sparerib recipes have you remove the membrane from the underside of the ribs before cooking them. I don't see the point: it's a pain in the ass to remove, and I like the extra structure that the membrane gives the rack.

SPARERIBS

MAKES 4 TO 6 SERVINGS

TWO 3-POUND RACKS ST. LOUIS–STYLE PORK SPARERIBS

1 CUP FETTE SAU DRY RUB (PAGE 22)

WOOD CHUNKS OR SOAKED WOOD CHIPS

① Put the ribs on a rimmed baking sheet and coat all over with the dry rub, patting it onto the surface until the meat has a thin, even layer of rub (you may not need all of the rub). Let the meat rest for 1 hour at room temperature, or until the rub starts to turn into a pasty coating.

② Preheat a smoker to 225°F or set up a grill for smoking (see page 13 or 16).

③ Place the racks of ribs, meaty side up, in the smoker and smoke, maintaining a smoker temperature of between 200° and 225°F, replenishing the charcoal and wood chunks or chips as needed.

④ After about 5 hours, start checking the ribs periodically: You should be able to easily tear a piece of meat from the bone with your fingers, but the meat shouldn't be falling-off-the-bone tender. An instant-read thermometer inserted in the center of the rib meat should register about 180°F. Total smoking time can be up to 7 hours.

⑤ Using tongs or a pair of heavy rubber gloves, transfer the racks to a cutting board and let rest for 10 minutes, then cut into individual ribs and serve, with sauce on the side, if you like.

PORK LOIN ROAST

A pork loin roast is the porcine version of prime rib, a cut that offers a bit of everything: loin muscle, tenderloin, loin, and baby back ribs. The presence of extra-lean meat warrants extra-careful attention to prevent it from drying out: this is one of the few times that I barbecue meat to temperature—rather than rely on texture—to know when it is done.

LOIN

Your butcher might offer to "French" the roast by removing the meat between the ribs. Tell her no thanks, that you're making barbecue and don't want to be robbed of the precious rib meat.

MAKES 8 SERVINGS

ONE 5- TO 6-POUND CENTER-CUT BONE-IN PORK LOIN ROAST (8 RIBS), CHINE BONE CRACKED OR REMOVED

1 CUP FETTE SAU DRY RUB (PAGE 22)

WOOD CHUNKS OR SOAKED WOOD CHIPS

❶ Put the roast on a rimmed baking sheet and coat all over with the dry rub, patting it onto the surface until the meat has an even layer of rub (you may not need all of the rub). If you have time, let the meat rest for 1 hour at room temperature, or until the rub starts to turn into a pasty coating.

❷ Preheat a smoker to 300°F or set up a grill for smoking (see page 13 or 16).

❸ Place the roast, rib side down, in the smoker and smoke, maintaining a smoker temperature of between 250° and 300°F, replenishing the charcoal and wood chunks or chips as needed.

❹ After about 2 hours, start checking the meat. The pork is done when an instant-read thermometer inserted into the center of the roast registers 140°F. Total smoking time can be up to 4 hours.

❺ Using tongs or a pair of heavy rubber gloves, transfer the roast to a cutting board and let rest for 10 minutes before cutting into individual ribs.

BEEF BRISKET

Brisket is the most difficult barbecue to get just right: There is a narrow window between the time when this tough, lean cut turns moist and tender and when it starts to dry out. To make matters worse, brisket comes in various weights and thicknesses and is often divided into two cuts by the butcher: the flat, or first cut, and the point, or second cut (also called the deckle), which is thicker, with a larger fat cap. Ideally you'll buy the biggest, fattiest, highest-grade whole brisket you can find, which will reduce your margin of error.

BRISKET

MAKES 10 TO 12 SERVINGS

**1 WHOLE BEEF BRISKET
(10 TO 14 POUNDS)**

1 CUP FETTE SAU DRY RUB (PAGE 22)

WOOD CHUNKS OR SOAKED WOOD CHIPS

❶ Trim the brisket's fat cap to about ¼ inch thick, removing any hard lumps of fat. Put it on a rimmed baking sheet and coat all over with the dry rub, patting it onto the surface until the meat has an even layer of rub (you may not need all of the rub). If you have time, let the meat rest for 1 hour at room temperature, or until the rub starts to turn into a pasty coating.

❷ Preheat a smoker to 225°F or set up a grill for smoking (see page 13 or 16).

❸ Place the brisket, fatty side up, in the smoker and smoke, maintaining a smoker temperature of between 210° and 225°F, replenishing the charcoal and wood chunks or chips as needed.

❹ After about 8 hours, start checking the meat periodically: Poke the brisket in a few places—the fat cap should be soft and pliant and the meat should separate under your finger. If you think your brisket is nearly finished, cut off a chunk and eat it. The bark should be dry and crisp, and the meat should be moist and tender but not mushy or overly chewy. An instant-read thermometer inserted into the center of the brisket should register about 185°F. Total smoking time can be 12 to 16 hours.

⑤ When your brisket is smoked to your liking, using two pairs of tongs or a pair of heavy rubber gloves, transfer it to a cutting board. If your cutting board doesn't have a channel for catching juices, put it on a rimmed baking sheet. Let the meat rest for at least 30 minutes.

⑥ Just before serving (once sliced, brisket dries out quickly), slice the brisket across the grain into ¼-inch pieces, beginning at the thinner end of the cut. When you encounter the thick band of tough fat that separates the point from the flat, cut the brisket into two pieces between the point and the flat. Remove most of the fat, then continue slicing and serve.

NOTE

Brisket is best eaten as soon as possible, but if you have to cook it ahead of time, let it cool to room temperature, then wrap it in multiple layers of plastic and refrigerate for up to 1 day. To rewarm the brisket, unwrap it and place it in a roasting pan. Add a splash of water and cover with foil, then heat it in a 200°F oven until warmed through. If the bark has gone soft, you can recrisp it over a medium-hot grill fire for a few minutes.

WOOD IS AN INGREDIENT

Barbecue isn't barbecue without wood smoke; wood is as much flavor as it is fuel, especially when you're cooking simple barbecue. When your only ingredients other than meat are dry rubs, or just salt and pepper, the type of wood you use can have a profound effect on the taste of the finished product.

I like to impart a good amount of smokiness to my barbecue, so whoever is eating it can smell and taste the smoke right away. Think of wood like a seasoning in the same way chefs use spices in their cooking. As with spices, you want to use enough to make its presence known but not so much that it overwhelms the dish.

CHOOSING WOOD

There are dozens of woods that can be used for barbecue and grilling. While it's true that each type produces its own unique flavor of smoke, the differences between one variety and the next can be subtle, especially when you are using them to smoke large cuts of meat already flavored with a spice rub.

Not all wood is meant for cooking. Anything with a high sap content—including pine, cedar, and other coniferous trees—should be avoided, as the sap will impart an unpleasant flavor (plus, some say the smoke from coniferous trees can make you sick). Conventional wisdom says that elm, eucalyptus, and sycamore are also unfit for smoking. Likewise, any green wood—that is, freshly cut wood that hasn't been properly seasoned (dried)—will contain too much moisture and sap, making it burn unevenly and sometimes imparting an unpleasant flavor. Always avoid scrap lumber, which might have been chemically treated or stained, as well as plywood.

The best wood for barbecuing and grilling has been either air-dried or seasoned in a kiln. The cheapest and most readily available wood will be whatever grows near you, but before you order from your local firewood supplier, ask them how their wood has been dried; many can sell you wood seasoned specifically for cooking. It's safe to assume that any wood chips or chunks you purchase by the bag at a retailer have been properly seasoned.

At home, you can experiment with various types of wood until you find one—or a combination of two or more woods—that best matches what you want to barbecue. To get you started, page 42 lists some of my favorites, arranged by their flavor from mildest to most assertive.

LOGS, CHUNKS, AND CHIPS

Wood used for barbecuing and grilling ranges from whole logs down to chips and pellets, which are made from pressurized sawdust for use in specialty smokers and grills. Most electric and propane smokers only work with wood chips, while charcoal smokers and grills can use wood in any form. A good rule of thumb is to use wood chunks for longer smoking times (2 or more hours) and chips for shorter ones. When barbecuing a large piece of meat, start with a few large chunks, then replenish the supply one or two pieces at a time to maintain a constant stream of smoke. Although whole logs are usually used only in large commercial smokers, you could keep a log fire burning next to your smoker and feed it with partially burned wood, which will provide both the heat of charcoal and the flavor of wood smoke.

TYPES OF WOOD AND THEIR FLAVORS

Mildest

ALDER: Often used to smoke fish (especially salmon), alder has a delicate and slightly sweet flavor.

ALMOND: Best used for seafood and poultry, almond wood produces a light, nutty-flavored smoke.

APPLE: The most popular of the "mild" woods, apple yields a sweet, fruity smoke flavor. It is most often used for pork and poultry, though it also works well as an all-around subtle wood for barbecue.

CHERRY: Cherry yields a sweet, fruity flavor; it will also impart a rosy hue to fish and poultry.

Moderate

GRAPE: If you live in or near wine country, you may be able to source dried grapevines for smoking, which will produce a tart, fruity flavor.

MAPLE: Maple has a lot of wood sugar, so it imparts sweeter flavors and aromas. It's great with poultry or pork barbecue that isn't aggressively seasoned.

SARSAPARILLA: Sarsaparilla is a musky-flavored wood that adds a mild root-beer note to poultry and game.

PECAN: Pecan wood gives off a flavor similar to hickory but is less intense. If you can get it, pecan makes a great all-around cooking wood.

Aggressive

OAK: The most versatile cooking wood, oak is dense and burns for a long time, making it ideal for smoking larger cuts of meat. Its flavor is strong but not so overpowering that you can't use it on seafood or poultry. Mix oak with other varieties of wood to create a more complex smoky flavor.

HICKORY: A popular all-around wood that's widely available, hickory has more punch than oak and a slightly nutty flavor. Many prefer hickory for pork and beef, and it can be used sparingly with poultry, in combination with other wood.

BEECH: Like oak, beech burns slowly and evenly with a moderately smoky flavor.

ACACIA: Acacia results in mesquite-like flavors, though much less intense and bitter.

Most Aggressive

PIMENTO: This exotic wood from Jamaican allspice trees is used for traditional jerk-style barbecue. It imparts a tangy, herbaceous flavor similar to that of its berries.

WALNUT: Walnut's hefty, deeply flavored smoke is best matched with big cuts of beef. It's often used in tandem with other milder woods.

MESQUITE: Although mesquite is popular and widely available, use it with caution: it can impart a pungent, bitter flavor that overpowers any cut of meat, especially when used as the only source of smoke. Even if you love that telltale mesquite flavor, it's best used in small amounts with other woods.

BEEF SHORT RIBS

Like brisket, short ribs have lots of connective tissue and need a long, slow spell in the smoker to turn tender. The meat on the exterior will be tender before the meat in the center of the ribs is ready. To make sure your ribs are tender all the way to the center, dig a little deeper when pulling a piece off to taste.

SHORT RIBS

MAKES 6 TO 8 SERVINGS

TWO 7-POUND RACKS BEEF SHORT RIBS
(4 BONES PER RACK)

1 CUP FETTE SAU DRY RUB (PAGE 22)

WOOD CHUNKS OR SOAKED WOOD
CHIPS

① Put the ribs on a rimmed baking sheet and coat all over with the dry rub, patting it onto the surface until the meat has an even layer of rub (you may not need all of the rub). If you have time, let the meat rest at room temperature for 1 hour, or until the rub starts to turn into a pasty coating.

② Preheat a smoker to 225°F or set up a grill for smoking (see page 13 or 16).

③ Put the racks of ribs, bone side down, in the smoker and smoke, maintaining a smoker temperature of between 210° and 225°F, replenishing the charcoal and wood chunks or chips as needed.

④ After about 4 hours, start checking the ribs periodically: You should be able to pull a piece of meat off the bone with your fingers. An instant-read thermometer inserted in the center of the rib meat should register about 180°F, and the meat should be tender all the way through. Total smoking time can be up to 6 hours.

⑤ Using tongs or a pair of heavy rubber gloves, transfer the racks to a cutting board and let rest for 10 minutes, then cut into individual ribs and serve, with sauce on the side, if desired.

LAMB SPARERIBS

If you like the flavor of lamb, you'll love lamb spareribs. They're fattier and less meaty than their pork counterparts, but they are smoked in the same manner. You'll notice a lot of external fat on the ribs; I like to leave all of it on to help keep the meat as moist as possible. You can always remove some of the fat after they're done or, better yet, crisp it up on a hot grill just before serving.

SPARERIBS

MAKES 4 SERVINGS

4 RACKS LAMB SPARERIBS (ABOUT 1½ POUNDS PER RACK)

1 CUP FETTE SAU DRY RUB (PAGE 22)

WOOD CHUNKS OR SOAKED WOOD CHIPS

❶ Put the ribs on a rimmed baking sheet and coat all over with the dry rub, patting it onto the surface until the meat has a thin, even layer of rub (you may not need all of the rub). If you have time, let the meat rest for 1 hour, or until the rub starts to turn into a pasty coating.

❷ Preheat a smoker to 225°F or set up a grill for smoking (see page 13 or 16).

❸ Place the racks of ribs, meaty side up, in the smoker and smoke, maintaining a smoker temperature of between 200°F and 225°F, replenishing the charcoal and wood chunks or chips as needed.

❹ After about 3 hours, start checking the ribs periodically: You should be able to easily tear a piece of meat off the bone with your fingers, but the meat shouldn't be falling-off-the-bone tender. An instant-read thermometer inserted in the center of the rib meat should register about 150°F. Total smoking time can be up to 5 hours.

❺ Using tongs or a pair of heavy rubber gloves, transfer the racks to a cutting board and let rest for 10 minutes, then cut into individual ribs and serve, with sauce on the side, if desired.

THE STALL

When barbecuing large cuts of meat like brisket or pork shoulder, you'll notice that the internal temperature rises quickly and constantly over the first few hours of smoking, then stalls somewhere between 150° and 170°F and hangs out there for a few hours before resuming its climb up the ladder. If you're monitoring the temperature of your meat as it cooks (which you don't really need to do), this can be a scary time. Don't worry: the "stall" is caused by moisture evaporating from the surface of the meat, which cools it down until all of the surface moisture has evaporated.

MOVING THE MEAT

Most of the time, you can set your meat in the smoker (always fattiest side up) and forget about it until it's finished. There's usually no need to move or turn it unless you notice parts of the cut beginning to burn (this usually happens around the edges)—this is a sign that your smoker has a hot spot. Simply rotate the grate or move the meat.

KNOWING WHEN IT'S DONE

Unless I'm smoking poultry, sausage, or cured meat, I rarely use a thermometer to check doneness when barbecuing (the opposite is true when I'm grilling; see page 84). With barbecue, texture is everything, and a thermometer can't help you with that. Barbecue is a lot like cooking pasta; you have to taste for doneness as it cooks, checking more frequently toward the end.

For beef (brisket, cheeks, and so on), the meat is done when you can easily rip off a piece with your fingers or a fork. Taste it; if it has the right amount of chew, it's done. How tender you like your meat is a matter of personal preference. With ribs, the meat should tear easily when you pull two bones apart.

The texture of the fat is just as important; you want it to feel like soft gelatin—almost liquid—when you poke it with your finger. It shouldn't spring back on you at all.

PULLED LEG OF GOAT

Although goat is the most widely consumed meat in the world, the demand in America is so low that most goat farmers here primarily raise the animals for milk and cheese. Many people say that goat is a very gamey meat, but I've always found its flavor to fall somewhere between that of beef and lamb. However, because it contains far less fat than other barbecue-bound animals, you have to pay attention and be sure to take it out of the smoker as soon as it's tender enough to pull, or it can be dry.

LEG

MAKES 8 TO 10 SERVINGS

ONE 5-POUND BONE-IN GOAT LEG
(SEE RESOURCES, PAGE 108)

1 CUP FETTE SAU DRY RUB (PAGE 22), PLUS (OPTIONAL) MORE FOR SEASONING

KOSHER SALT (OPTIONAL)

POTATO ROLLS OR HAMBURGER BUNS, FOR SERVING

WOOD CHUNKS OR SOAKED WOOD CHIPS

① Put the goat leg on a rimmed baking sheet and generously cover it with the dry rub, making sure to stuff and pat the rub into any cracks and crevices in the meat. If you have time, let the meat rest for 1 hour at room temperature, or until the rub starts to moisten and turn into a pasty coating.

② Preheat a smoker to 225°F or set up a grill for smoking (see page 13 or 16).

③ Place the goat in the smoker and smoke, maintaining a smoker temperature of between 200° and 225°F, replenishing the charcoal and wood chunks or chips as needed.

④ After about 4 hours, begin checking the goat periodically: When it's done, you should be able to easily pull a hunk of meat off with your fingers and the exterior should have a thick, chewy bark. An instant-read thermometer inserted in the center of the meat should register about 150°F. Total smoking time can be up to 8 hours.

⑤ Using heavy rubber gloves, transfer the leg to a rimmed baking sheet and let it rest for at least 30 minutes.

⑥ Begin pulling the goat into pieces. As you pull the meat, discard any large pieces of fat that you come across.

⑦ Once all the goat is pulled, taste a piece and, if necessary, season the meat with salt or dry rub. Serve with potato rolls or hamburger buns.

NOTE

To rewarm the goat, put it in a roasting pan or casserole, add a splash of barbecue sauce, vinegar, or water, and cover with a lid or foil. Rewarm in a 250°F oven.

THE SMOKE RING

Much has been made of the smoke ring, a band of pinkish meat found directly below the bark in many kinds of barbecue. Some mistake it for undercooked meat, but it's actually the result of a chemical reaction between dissolved smoke gases and meat juice that prevents the meat from turning gray. If your 'cue doesn't have a smoke ring, don't worry: it probably just means you should add more smoke next time.

SAUCES

G ood barbecue should be able to stand on its own. But barbecue sauce has become the *definition* of barbecue for many people, who think that slathering a piece of meat with a shiny red condiment turns it into barbecue. This couldn't be farther from the truth. Too much great barbecue is ruined by being drowned in sauce before being served—just as so much truly awful barbecue attempts to hide itself in a bath of the stuff.

That said, I know that many people love barbecue sauce. So here are three styles of sauce: a sweet tomato-based barbecue sauce, a spicy sauce made with pureed chile peppers, and a vinegar sauce made with cider. These sauces can be used interchangeably with any style of 'cue, though most folks pair the sweet and spicy sauces (or a combination thereof) with smoked beef and poultry and the vinegar sauce with pork.

Sauce is one of the few ways you can put your personal stamp on your 'cue. It's also the defining characteristic of many regional barbecue styles. In eastern North Carolina, smoked hogs are served with a dressing of vinegar and red pepper flakes, while in the western part of the state, a touch of tomato is added to the vinegary base for its pulled pork shoulders. South Carolina's "mustard belt" takes its name from the intense mustard sauce used to dress its pork barbecue. The funky Worcestershire-based "dip" of western Kentucky is a natural pairing for the region's mutton barbecue. Memphis serves its famous ribs doused with a thin tomato and vinegar sauce. Kansas City 'cue is usually paired with a thick, sweet tomato sauce, and the legendary Alabama joint Big Bob Gibson's popularized a ranch dressing–like sauce that now pervades the state.

SWEET BARBECUE SAUCE

A sweet molassesy tomato-based sauce is what comes to mind when most people think of barbecue. This version has an equal balance of sweet, savory, and acid. The Worcestershire sauce goes a long way in taming the sweetness of the ketchup, and the beer, cider, and vinegar add enough zip to tie everything together.

MAKES ABOUT 2 CUPS

2 CUPS KETCHUP

3 TABLESPOONS WORCESTERSHIRE SAUCE

2 TABLESPOONS CIDER VINEGAR

2 TABLESPOONS HARD CIDER

2 TABLESPOONS PILSNER BEER

2 TABLESPOONS DARK BROWN SUGAR

2 TEASPOONS COLMAN'S MUSTARD POWDER (SEE NOTE, PAGE 96)

½ TEASPOON GARLIC POWDER

½ TEASPOON CAYENNE PEPPER

1 TEASPOON KOSHER SALT

1 In a large nonreactive saucepan, combine all the ingredients, bring to a simmer, and cook, whisking occasionally, for 45 minutes. The sauce will thicken and darken as it cooks.

2 Let cool. Transfer the sauce to a container, cover, and refrigerate until ready to use. The sauce can be refrigerated for up to 1 month (but if you add meat juices, discard it after a couple of days).

VINEGAR SAUCE

This vinegar sauce works equally well with all kinds of smoked meat—not just the pork it's often paired with. This sauce will add brightness to pulled pork, and it has enough depth to stand up to beef and lamb.

MAKES ABOUT 2½ CUPS

2 CUPS CIDER VINEGAR

½ CUP WORCESTERSHIRE SAUCE

2 TABLESPOONS DARK BROWN SUGAR

1 TABLESPOON HARD CIDER

1½ TEASPOONS KOSHER SALT

1½ TEASPOONS COLMAN'S MUSTARD POWDER (SEE NOTE, PAGE 96)

⅛ TEASPOON CAYENNE PEPPER

⅛ TEASPOON GARLIC POWDER

⅛ TEASPOON GRANULATED ONION

① In a large nonreactive saucepan, combine all the ingredients and bring to a boil, then turn off the heat and let cool to room temperature.

② Transfer the sauce to a container, cover, and refrigerate until ready to use. The sauce can be refrigerated for up to 1 week.

MAKING BOTTLED SAUCE BETTER

As you'll see in these recipes, a decent barbecue sauce doesn't take long to make. But unlike chicken stock or marinara, homemade sauce isn't always better. There are a surprising number of good bottled sauces out there. And there's no harm in tweaking a store-bought sauce: you can play with acidity and heat by adding vinegar and hot sauce or add some savory depth with Worcestershire sauce or drippings left over from the meat.

SPICY CHILE PEPPER SAUCE

Warning: this sauce—which is basically pureed chiles, seeds and all—lives up to its name. But it's not a simple, one-note hot sauce; the combination of three chiles gives it a great depth of rich, smoky flavor. Though folks who love a lot of heat with their 'cue use this sauce straight, you can combine it in equal parts with Sweet Barbecue Sauce (page 51), which results in the perfect balance of sweet and spicy.

MAKES ABOUT 2 CUPS

2 OUNCES DRIED PASILLA CHILES (ABOUT 7 CHILES), STEMMED

2 OUNCES CHIPOTLE CHILES (ABOUT 20 CHILES)

½ OUNCE DRIED CHILES DE ÁRBOL (ABOUT 30 CHILES)

2 GARLIC CLOVES, SMASHED AND PEELED

1 SMALL YELLOW ONION, THINLY SLICED

8 CUPS WATER

1 TEASPOON KOSHER SALT

1 TEASPOON GARLIC POWDER

1 TEASPOON GROUND CUMIN

2 TEASPOONS CIDER VINEGAR

① In a large saucepan, combine the chiles, garlic, onion, and water and bring to a boil, then lower the heat and simmer, uncovered, for 1 hour.

② Strain the cooking liquid into a bowl and transfer the contents of the strainer to a blender. Add 1 cup of the reserved cooking liquid, the salt, garlic powder, cumin, and vinegar and blend on high speed until pureed.

③ Pass the chile puree through a fine-mesh strainer into a bowl, pressing on the solids. The sauce should be the consistency of ketchup; add a splash of water if it's too thick. Let cool.

④ Transfer the sauce to a container, cover, and refrigerate until ready to use. The sauce can be refrigerated for up to 4 days.

SPICY MUSTARD

This simple homemade mustard is definitely not a French-style mustard sauce. It's most akin to hot Chinese mustard, which is also made from mustard powder. Make sure you use Colman's mustard powder here; the generic powder sold in the spice section is too weak.

You'll find that this mustard is especially pungent at first, but the flavor mellows over time. You can make the sauce with your favorite beer; feel free to experiment. Anything that's not very hoppy should work well.

MAKES A SCANT 2 CUPS

ONE 12-OUNCE BOTTLE LAGER OR ALE

ONE 4-OUNCE CONTAINER COLMAN'S MUSTARD POWDER

Pour the beer into a large jar and let the foam settle. Add the mustard powder, seal the jar, and shake well. The sauce will keep indefinitely in the refrigerator, though the flavor will mellow over time.

GRILLED

There are dozens of beef, pork, and lamb cuts appropriate for grilling. But before grilling any piece of red meat, you should know what you're dealing with and adjust your grilling method accordingly. Meat with lots of intramuscular fat—like a beef rib-eye steak or lamb loin chop—is best seared first to get a deep char, then cooked to temperature over lower heat. Thick but lean cuts that carry most of their fat on the outside—like pork chops—benefit from brining or marinating, which helps keep the interior moist as you char the outside. Leaner meats with little marbling or external fat—like veal, beef rump steak, or pork cutlets—should be grilled quickly over a hot fire; by the time they take on a good char, they'll be cooked through.

That char is the secret to great grilling, and is something only a hot grill can deliver. It can transform an ordinary piece of meat into something deeply primal tasting, with a textural harmony that drives carnivores crazy: a crunchy, burnished crust and a juicy, tender interior.

Unfortunately, most cooks are afraid to give food the char it deserves. They equate char with burnt food, but the two are distinctly different: Burnt food is completely carbonized and tastes acrid and unpleasant. Char is deep caramelization on a food's surface, that smoky-sweet flavor we associate with live-fire cooking; without it, you might as well stand at the stove.

People also get too hung up on creating perfect crosshatched grill marks on their meat. While this looks great in photographs, they're missing out on a lot of surface area that could be charred; this is why I prefer to move and turn meat frequently while making sure that as much of its surface touches the hot grill grates as possible. A steak charred all over tastes significantly better than one with a few black stripes. And this flavor gets even better when you add charcoal to the equation.

When it comes to chicken, leave the breast on the bone, and do the same with any other piece of chicken too. Cooking chicken on the bone both helps the meat hold its shape and prevents it from drying out, and removing the skin both exposes the chicken to more moisture loss and robs you of a delicacy: crispy skin is the best part about eating the bird, no?

Grilling chicken is a race against the clock: the challenge is always to get the meat cooked through before it begins to dry out. White meat (breasts) takes less time to cook than dark meat (legs and thighs). You can, of course, cook breasts and legs separately, but when you want to grill a whole chicken, butterfly it first—that is, remove the backbone with a pair of heavy kitchen shears. Opening the chicken out on the grill not only makes for a more uniform thickness, it also shortens the cooking time and exposes more skin to the hot surface, ensuring that the entire exterior will be crispy by the time the bird is cooked through. But before we get ahead of ourselves, we need to choose a grill.

CHOOSE YOUR GRILL

Gas or charcoal? Choosing a grill begins with the all-important question of fuel. While you can make the recipes in this book using a gas grill, grill pan, or, hell, even a George Foreman "grill," grilling without charcoal is like playing bluegrass without a banjo: something will be unmistakably absent. I've already emphasized the importance of using hardwood charcoal when barbecuing—there's no substitute for the flavor it adds to smoked meat. The same goes for grilling. While it's true that nothing can compete with the convenience of a gas grill, it's also true that nothing can compete with the flavor of charcoal-grilled food.

GAS GRILLS

Gas grills can be lit with the push of a button and are ready to start cooking in a few minutes, and you never have to worry about tending a fire or adding more fuel (until the propane tank runs out). The cooking temperature is both more consistent and easier to adjust with gas, you can easily create two or more heat zones, and there is far less cleanup when you're finished. Many gas grills also have neat accessories and add-ons, like side burners, warming racks, and rotisseries. For all of these reasons, most home cooks opt for gas grills.

However, gas grills lose out to charcoal in two important categories: First, most gas grills can't get nearly as hot as even the cheapest charcoal grill, which means food won't get enough char before it's cooked through. A commercial gas grill can get as hot as charcoal, yes, but most of the four-wheeled contraptions sitting on our decks and patios don't come close. More important, you're missing out on a key ingredient when you cook with gas: charcoal. Carbonized wood is more than just fuel. It imparts its own flavor: a smokiness we associate with backyard cookouts, feasts on the beach, summertime gatherings, and a host of other food memories. The smoke produced by burning charcoal is different from that produced by burning gas: Gas smoke is basically flavorless, whereas charcoal smoke contains more compounds that contribute flavor.

If a gas grill makes more sense for you, though, buy one! What you might lose in flavor you'll make up for in speed and ease.

CHARCOAL GRILLS

Grilling over charcoal has a visceral appeal—think of steaks sizzling over a pile of glowing, smoldering coals—that a gas grill can't match. And charcoal grills are far cheaper than gas ones. Your main consideration when choosing a charcoal grill should be size: it should be able to accommodate two or more heat zones, a setup that's needed (or at least helpful) for cooking many of the recipes in this book. For kettle grills, look for a diameter of 20 inches or larger; most barrel- or box-shaped charcoal grills are wide enough for multistage grilling. If you plan to barbecue on your grill, bigger is better, so the meat won't be too close to the heat source.

You can actually eliminate the need for multizone cooking by using a charcoal grill that lets you raise and lower the grate over the coals to fine-tune the cooking temperature. Argentinean-style grills (see Resources, page 108), which are in this category, are operated by crank. A simpler style of adjustable grill is the Tuscan grill (see Resources), which has a grate that can rest on two or three different levels of rungs. The best thing about a Tuscan grill is its portability.

Your next consideration should be the grilling grate itself. I prefer a standard wire grate to wide metal or cast-iron bars: more space between the bars allows more airflow and more direct heat to reach your food, which helps brown the entire surface, not just what's touching the grate. You should also look for grates that have hinged sections that allow you to add or move charcoal and wood without having to remove the entire grate.

Two more essentials: The grill should have two vents—one in the base and one in the lid—for controlling airflow and, thus, heat. And it should have enough headspace to accommodate large pieces of meat or whole poultry when the grill is covered.

Beyond that, choose a model that suits your individual needs and budget. My workhorse is the Weber One-Touch, a simple kettle grill that cost about $100 and has never failed me.

ORGANIZE YOUR EQUIPMENT

There's an entire industry built around grilling gadgets (what else are we supposed to get our dads for Father's Day?). But you need only a few simple tools to get you on the path to grilling greatness.

CHIMNEY STARTER

A charcoal fire begins with a chimney starter (see page 70). Better yet, buy two of them: one to fill your grill with an initial load of coals and another to keep extra coals ready for replenishing, or to dump two loads of charcoal into the grill for an extra-hot fire.

INSTANT-READ THERMOMETER

If you want to cook meat properly, you need a reliable thermometer—there's just no way around it. Buy the fastest and most accurate thermometer you can afford. My favorite, the ThermoWorks Thermapen, runs around $100 but pays for itself quickly when you consider how many expensive pieces of meat it will prevent you from overcooking. There are cheaper instant-read thermometers on the market, but whatever you buy, check its speed and accuracy by testing it in a pot of boiling water: it should register 212°F within a few seconds. If it doesn't, get a better thermometer.

WIRE BRUSH

A stiff wire brush will help you clean your grates before and after grilling. Look for one with a long, sturdy handle and a built-in scraper for tackling any stuck food particles. Brush the grates once they have heated up, then grab a rolled-up towel or wad of paper towels with a pair of tongs, dip it in water, and wipe the grates clean before oiling the grates and cooking. Repeat this process after you've finished grilling to keep the grates gunk- and rust-free.

TONGS

Most tongs designed for grilling are worthlessly flimsy. Long-handled, V-shaped, spring-loaded kitchen tongs are much better. Keep at least two pairs handy whenever you grill: one for handling charcoal and lifting the grate and another for moving food around on the grill.

HEAVY-DUTY GLOVES

I keep a pair of heavy rubber gloves handy whenever I'm smoking or grilling larger pieces of meat that can't be easily moved with tongs. Fireproof leather gloves are also handy for handling hot chimney starters and for shielding your hands from heat when brushing food or moving it around the grill.

BASTING BRUSH

I don't do a ton of basting when I grill meat, but for recipes that do require basting or brushing, a long-handled brush with silicone bristles is best: the bristles won't catch fire and they can be cleaned more easily than natural bristles.

SPRAY BOTTLE

A few flames licking at your food is fine, but especially fatty meats will create the occasional flare-up, which can scorch your food and make it taste burnt. A cheap spray bottle will extinguish any flare-ups; use one with an adjustable nozzle set to the thinnest stream possible.

ASH CAN

Ashes are a grill's worst enemy. They absorb heat, get blown onto food, and, if they get wet, turn into cement that is hard to remove. Always remove any leftover coals and ashes after you've finished grilling and dump them into a metal ash can with a lid. Once they are completely cool, the ashes can be dumped into the trash.

GRILL COVER

An uncovered grill will quickly become a rusty, ruined one. Buy a cover that will shield it from the elements.

AXE-HANDLE RIB-EYE STEAK

When cooking a Flintstones-size steak like this, sear it first to make sure it gets enough char, then grill it to temperature over low heat. You can also cook the steak over low heat until it reaches 115°F (for medium-rare) and let it rest until you're ready to finish it off, then quickly grill it over scorching-high heat until it's charred all over and serve it immediately.

RIB-EYE STEAK

MAKES 2 TO 4 SERVINGS

ONE AXE-HANDLE RIB-EYE STEAK (2½ TO 3¾ POUNDS), ABOUT 2 INCHES THICK

KOSHER SALT AND FRESHLY GROUND BLACK PEPPER

¼ CUP MELTED GARLIC BUTTER (PAGE 66) OR 4 TABLESPOONS UNSALTED BUTTER, MELTED

FLAKY SEA SALT, SUCH AS MALDON

❶ Prepare a two-stage fire with high and low sides in a grill (see page 71). Have a spray bottle handy to extinguish any large flare-ups; it's OK for flames to lick the steak now and then, but they shouldn't slobber it with kisses.

❷ Shower the steak with kosher salt and pepper very generously. Grill the steak over high heat, moving it and turning it every minute or so, until it's well charred on both sides and around the perimeter, 8 to 10 minutes.

❸ Move the steak to the low-heat side of the grill and cook until an instant-read thermometer inserted into the center of the meat registers 125°F for medium-rare, 20 to 30 minutes, depending on the size of your steak. Transfer the steak to a platter and let rest for 10 minutes.

❹ If the surface of the steak is moist with juices after resting, quickly sear the steak on both sides over high heat to crisp up the crust, about 30 seconds per side. Transfer the steak to a platter.

❺ Carve the steak into portions by first cutting the meat away from the bone, then carving the steak across the grain into large pieces. Serve with the melted butter and flaky salt on the side.

BUTCHER'S STEAKS WITH GARLIC BUTTER

The hanger steak (aka butcher's steak) is one of the most underrated cuts of beef. It's silky and fairly tender. On the grill, treat this long, irregularly shaped cut like a sausage, turning it frequently to get a good char on all sides. Try it cooked to medium, which makes it a bit more tender than medium-rare while retaining its gamey flavor and buttery texture.

HANGER STEAK

MAKES 4 SERVINGS

FOUR 10-OUNCE HANGER STEAKS, TRIMMED

KOSHER SALT AND FRESHLY GROUND BLACK PEPPER

6 TABLESPOONS MELTED GARLIC BUTTER (RECIPE FOLLOWS)

COARSE SEA SALT

❶ Prepare a hot single-level fire in a grill (see page 71).

❷ Generously season the steaks with kosher salt and pepper. Grill the steaks, turning frequently, for about 8 minutes for medium-rare or 10 minutes for medium. Transfer to a cutting board and let rest for 5 minutes.

❸ Cut the steaks across the grain on the diagonal into 1-inch slices. Divide among four plates, drizzle with the garlic butter, and sprinkle with coarse salt. Serve.

GARLIC BUTTER

Makes about 1 cup

½ POUND (2 STICKS) UNSALTED BUTTER, CUBED

6 GARLIC CLOVES, FINELY CHOPPED

① In a saucepan, melt the butter over low heat. Add the garlic and cook over medium-low heat for 5 minutes; the butter should simmer gently but not brown. Remove from the heat.

② Skim the foam from the top of the butter and slowly pour the butter through a fine-mesh strainer set over a bowl. Discard the milky solids and garlic. The butter can be refrigerated for up to 3 weeks.

NEW YORK STRIP STEAKS WITH SAUCE AU POIVRE

Despite its band of external fat, strip steak itself isn't terrifically marbled. The texture falls somewhere between that of buttery tenderloin and chewier rib eye—as does the intensity of its flavor. The sauce is proof that pepper brings out the best in red meat.

STRIP STEAKS

MAKES 4 SERVINGS

1 TABLESPOON EXTRA-VIRGIN OLIVE OIL

2 TABLESPOONS VERY FINELY CHOPPED SHALLOTS

1½ TEASPOONS COARSELY GROUND BLACK PEPPER, OR MORE TO TASTE

2 TABLESPOONS APPLE BRANDY

2 CUPS HEAVY CREAM

1 TABLESPOON PINK PEPPERCORNS

KOSHER SALT AND FRESHLY GROUND BLACK PEPPER

FOUR 13-OUNCE STRIP STEAKS, ABOUT 2 INCHES THICK

❶ Prepare a two-stage fire with high and medium-low sides in a grill (see page 71).

❷ Meanwhile, in a medium skillet, heat the olive oil over medium-low heat. Add the shallots and cook until translucent, about 5 minutes. Add the coarsely ground black pepper and brandy and carefully tilt the pan slightly away from yourself to ignite the brandy (if you're using an electric stove, carefully light the brandy with a match or a lighter), then cook until the flames subside.

❸ Add the cream and pink peppercorns, bring to a simmer, and reduce by half. Season the sauce with more coarsely ground pepper and salt and keep warm over low heat until ready to serve.

❹ Season the steaks generously with salt and freshly ground pepper. Grill the steaks over high heat, turning every couple of minutes, until well charred on both sides, 10 to 12 minutes. Transfer the steaks to the medium-low side of the grill and cook until an instant-read thermometer inserted horizontally into the middle of the steaks reads 135°F for medium, 10 to 15 minutes longer.

❺ Transfer the steaks to plates and let rest for 5 minutes, then serve with the warm sauce.

BEER-MARINATED RUMP STEAKS

RUMP STEAKS

This recipe is inspired by a technique from an ancient Northern Italian recipe for meat marinated in wine and spices for an extended period of time—up to 1 week. I took the idea and made a British version, marinating rump steaks, also known as top round steaks here in the United States, in English imperial stout with spices and citrus zest.

Beerwise, any higher-alcohol full-bodied English stout or porter will work, but my favorite for this marinade is imperial stout (aka imperial Russian stout). It's dark and robust, usually with an alcohol content of about 9 percent ABV.

MAKES 4 SERVINGS

4 RUMP (TOP ROUND) STEAKS
(ABOUT 8 OUNCES EACH)

24 OUNCES (3 CUPS) IMPERIAL STOUT
OR OTHER FULL-BODIED DARK BEER

½ TEASPOON GROUND CINNAMON

½ TEASPOON FRESHLY GRATED
NUTMEG

KOSHER SALT AND FRESHLY GROUND
BLACK PEPPER

3 LONG STRIPS ORANGE ZEST

1 Put the steaks in a large resealable plastic bag. Pour the beer into a bowl and, when the foam subsides, whisk in the cinnamon, nutmeg, and ½ teaspoon each salt and pepper. Pour the marinade into the bag, adding as much as necessary to completely cover the steaks, add the orange zest, and seal the bag tightly, squeezing out any extra air as you go. Refrigerate the steaks for 2 to 3 days.

2 Prepare a two-stage fire with medium and low sides in a grill (see page 71).

3 Remove the steaks from the bag; discard the marinade. Pat the steaks very dry with paper towels and season generously with salt and pepper. Grill the steaks over the medium side of the grill, moving and turning them every couple of minutes, until an instant-read thermometer inserted into the middle reads 135°F for medium, 8 to 10 minutes. If the steaks are charred before they're ready, move them to the low side.

4 Let the steaks rest for 5 minutes before serving.

CHARCOAL: KEEP IT PURE

U se hardwood charcoal for grilling, often in concert with hardwood chunks or wood chips, to add more wood-smoke flavor. Pure hardwood charcoal is black, chalky, and irregularly shaped. It's made by slowly burning wood in a controlled low-oxygen environment until it's almost completely carbonized. When lit, these lumps burn cleanly and evenly and impart a bit of smoky flavor to food. Hardwood charcoal burns faster than briquettes, as it's less compact, so you'll need to replenish the coals more often if grilling for longer periods of time. Although you can sometimes find hardwood charcoal made from a specific wood, most is made from scrap wood of unknown provenance. I haven't found "varietal" charcoal to contribute any noticeable flavor difference, though charcoal that is all made from the same type of wood probably burns more evenly and consistently than charcoal made from assorted scraps.

Most backyard cooks still use charcoal briquettes. Briquettes are made by burning sawdust and wood chips, then mixing the carbonized wood with binders and additives and molding them into uniformly shaped pillows. The "other" stuff in charcoal briquettes varies from one brand to the next, but it often includes sodium nitrate, mineral coal, starch, and fresh sawdust. The main advantage briquettes have over lump charcoal is the consistency at which they burn, which is more slowly and more evenly than hardwood. Briquettes also produce a lot more ash, which can insulate the coals and lower their heat output. I prefer hardwood charcoal to briquettes; the flavor is more pure and natural and there's a lot less mystery. Whichever you choose, stay far away from any briquettes impregnated with lighter fluid or other accelerants; these will definitely add nasty flavors to your food.

Before we bought our fuel charcoal in paper bags, we Americans simply burned logs down into coals, then grilled over them. That is still the best fuel for grilling by far, though it's also the least practical and most time-consuming: not only do you know exactly where your fuel comes from, you will also get more wood-smoke flavor. Making your own coals is as easy as building a fire in your grill and waiting until the logs become coals.

BUILDING A CHARCOAL FIRE

If you have a chimney starter, begin by loosely crumpling up a couple of sheets of newspaper and drizzling or spraying them with vegetable oil (this will make them burn longer and will speed up the charcoal lighting process). Stuff the newspaper into the lower chamber. Remove the grill's top grate (where the food will be placed) and set it aside; put the chimney starter on the grill's bottom grate. Fill it with charcoal, light the newspaper, and let the charcoal burn until the coals are glowing red and coated in gray ash, about 15 minutes. (You can speed the process by blowing on the chimney with a hair dryer; the extra air flow will make the coals ignite more quickly.) Carefully dump the charcoal onto the bottom grate into your desired arrangement (see Arranging the Charcoal, below), then replace the top grate.

If you don't have a chimney starter, remove the grill's bottom grate and place some crumpled newspaper in the bottom of the grill. Drizzle the paper with vegetable oil, cover it with the grate, and add a pile of charcoal. Light the newspaper and let the charcoal burn until it's covered in gray ash, then scatter it into your desired arrangement.

Once you have a layer of glowing coals in your grill, you can add another layer of unlit charcoal on top. You'll want to do this when using a large or deep kettle grill or when you want to create a deeper bed of coals for hotter direct-heat grilling. Then wait until the new charcoal has ignited before grilling. If you're using hardwood charcoal, you can throw a few lumps onto burning coals anytime during the grilling process. With briquettes, be sure to let them ignite and burn until they're ashen (to burn off the bad-tasting chemicals) before cooking over them.

I've also used a chimney starter as a makeshift grill by placing a grate directly on top of the burning coals. This is good for quickly searing a tuna steak or any other protein that you only want to char on the outside without cooking the interior.

ARRANGING THE CHARCOAL

There are numerous ways to set up a charcoal fire, depending on what you're cooking and how much heat you need. Create two zones for grilling: a hot or medium-hot side for searing and charring food and a low-heat or completely cool (charcoal-free) side for cooking thicker cuts of meat and indirect grilling.

SINGLE-LEVEL FIRE

Spread an even layer of charcoal, about one or two coals deep, over the bottom of the grill. This will create a medium- to medium-hot fire, depending on the thickness of the coals, that is best for direct cooking of ingredients that would burn over a hotter fire, such as vegetables and fish. If you are cooking thinner cuts of meat or other foods that need only a quick spell on the grill, you can make a deeper bed of coals to create a scorching-hot fire.

TWO-STAGE FIRE

You can create two heat zones by adding different amounts of coals to each side of the grill (or leaving one half of the grill coal-free to create a cool side). For a hot zone, build a layer about two coals deep; for medium, one coal deep; for low, scatter a few coals evenly over that side; and for cool, use no coals at all.

MULTI-ZONE FIRE

If you have a large rectangular grill or large kettle grill, you can make hot, medium, and low zones by making two separate layers of coals (about two coals deep for high heat and a single layer of coals for medium) and leaving a third section devoid of charcoal. Use this setup when grilling a variety of foods at the same time.

BUTTER-POACHED AND GRILLED BEEF TENDERLOIN STEAKS

Beef tenderloin (aka filet mignon) is unmatched in tenderness, but beyond that, it's a pretty boring cut of beef. It has a mild flavor and is practically devoid of fat, so you really need to do something dramatic to make it worth your trouble (and money). When I ran across Thomas Keller's recipe for *beurre monté*—an emulsification of butter and a little water that can be warmed to higher temperatures than plain butter without breaking—I thought it would be perfect on tenderloin. Poach the beef tenderloin steaks in butter until cooked to rare, then finish them over the hottest fire you can build in your grill. The result: a soft-as-ever meat with a crackling-crisp exterior and extra-buttery interior.

TENDERLOIN
STEAKS

MAKES 4 SERVINGS

2 TABLESPOONS WATER

1 POUND (4 STICKS) COLD UNSALTED BUTTER, CUT INTO TABLESPOON-SIZE PIECES

4 BEEF TENDERLOIN STEAKS (ABOUT 6 OUNCES EACH)

KOSHER SALT AND COARSELY GROUND BLACK PEPPER

① In a medium saucepan, bring the water to a boil. Reduce the heat to very low and slowly whisk in the butter a tablespoon at a time, adding another piece only once the previous one has emulsified. The butter will start to look glossy and like hollandaise; if it begins to bubble, remove the pan from the heat to cool slightly before continuing.

② Once all of the butter has been emulsified, add the beef. Use an instant-read or candy thermometer to monitor the *beurre monté*'s temperature: you want to keep it between 140° and 150°F, and you may have to turn off the heat from time to time to prevent it from getting too hot. Cook the beef until an instant-read thermometer inserted horizontally into the center reads 120°F, 20 to 30 minutes. If the beef isn't completely submerged in the butter, turn it over after 10 minutes.

③ Meanwhile, prepare a hot single-level fire in a grill (see page 71).

④ Remove the beef from the *beurre monté*, letting the excess butter drip off, and transfer to a plate. Season the beef with salt and pepper. Grill the steaks, turning once, until charred and cooked to the desired doneness, about 1 minute per side for medium-rare. Transfer to plates and serve.

NOTE

The leftover *beurre monté* can be used to poach other meat and seafood. Discard after 1 day.

HOW HOT IS THE GRILL?

There's no foolproof way to measure the heat of a charcoal fire. Even the most precise thermometers can only check the temperature of a specific spot, and even a perfectly uniform bed of coals will result in a range of constantly fluctuating temperatures as they burn, creating hotter and cooler spots above.

However, you've probably come across the "hand test," in which you place your paw a few inches over the fire and count until the heat becomes unbearably painful. Fun, right? There are many reasons why the hand test is an inaccurate gauge of temperature at best and self-inflicted torture at worst. That said, the hand test is, unfortunately, your best bet until you

get accustomed to how much heat a given charcoal arrangement will produce. Just before you're ready to put the food on the grill, place your hand about 5 inches above the grate and count—or, better yet, look at your watch (we tend to count more quickly when our flesh is hovering over a scorching-hot fire). See how long you can comfortably hold your hand over the heat to determine how hot the fire is.

8-plus seconds = low heat

6 to 8 seconds = medium-low

4 to 6 seconds = medium

2 to 4 seconds = medium-hot

Less than 2 seconds = hot

LAMB SADDLE CHOPS WITH MINT-YOGURT SAUCE

The lamb saddle chop (aka double loin chop or English chop) is an especially succulent (read: fatty) cut that combines the loin and tenderloin, usually with two fatty curlicues hanging off the edges. Most lamb cuts are small and dainty; saddle cut chops have the same intimidating presence on the plate as a huge steak.

SADDLE CHOPS

MAKES 4 SERVINGS

¾ CUP GREEK YOGURT

¼ CUP EXTRA-VIRGIN OLIVE OIL

2 TABLESPOONS CIDER VINEGAR

2 TEASPOONS DIJON MUSTARD

2 TEASPOONS SUGAR

¼ CUP FINELY CHOPPED MINT

KOSHER SALT AND FRESHLY GROUND BLACK PEPPER

4 LAMB SADDLE CHOPS
(15 TO 20 OUNCES EACH)

❶ Prepare a two-stage fire with medium and low sides in a grill (see page 71).

❷ In a small bowl, whisk the yogurt, olive oil, cider vinegar, mustard, sugar, and mint until combined. Season the sauce with salt and pepper. Refrigerate until ready to serve; the sauce can be refrigerated for up to 1 day.

❸ Generously season the lamb all over with salt and pepper. Grill the lamb over medium heat, turning frequently, until well charred on all sides; make sure to grill the fatty edges long enough to render some fat and get them very crisp. Move the lamb to the low side of the grill and cook until an instant-read thermometer inserted into the thickest part of the meat registers 140°F for medium, 15 to 20 minutes. Transfer the lamb to a plate and let rest for at least 5 minutes.

❹ Transfer the lamb to plates, spoon some of the yogurt sauce over the chops, and serve.

LAMB SHOULDER BLADE CHOPS WITH MINT-GREMOLATA BUTTER

The blade chop isn't a cut for beginners: you either have to love eating fat or have a surgeon's knife skills for working your way around it. Either way, you'll be rewarded with one of the juiciest and most intensely flavored (and most economical) cuts of lamb.

SHOULDER BLADE
CHOPS

MAKES 4 SERVINGS

FOUR 14-OUNCE LAMB SHOULDER BLADE CHOPS

KOSHER SALT AND FRESHLY GROUND BLACK PEPPER

FOUR ½-INCH DISKS MINT-GREMOLATA BUTTER (RECIPE FOLLOWS)

❶ Prepare a hot single-level fire in a grill (see page 71).

❷ Season the lamb chops generously with salt and pepper. Grill, turning once or twice, until well charred and cooked to the desired doneness, 8 to 10 minutes for medium. Transfer the lamb chops to plates.

❸ Place a disk of butter on top of each lamb chop. Let the lamb rest for 5 minutes before serving.

MINT-GREMOLATA BUTTER

Makes about ½ pound

½ POUND (2 STICKS) UNSALTED BUTTER, AT ROOM TEMPERATURE

¼ CUP FINELY CHOPPED MINT

FINELY CHOPPED ZEST OF 2 LEMONS (ABOUT ¼ CUP)

1 TABLESPOON HONEY

1 TEASPOON KOSHER SALT

½ TEASPOON FRESHLY GROUND BLACK PEPPER

In a food processor, combine the butter, mint, lemon zest, honey, salt, and pepper and pulse until well combined. Transfer the butter mixture to a sheet of plastic wrap and, using the plastic wrap, form it into a log about 2 inches thick. Twist the ends tightly to seal and refrigerate until firm. (The gremolata butter can be refrigerated for up to 1 week or frozen for up to 1 month. Defrost before using.)

SWEET TEA-BRINED POUSSINS

Poussin is a term for a young chicken, about a month old and weighing in at around a pound. These birds are perfect for grilling: their small, single-serving size makes them cook rather quickly, which keeps the meat moist and tender. If you can't find poussins (or spring chickens, as they're sometimes called) at your market or butcher, grab a Cornish game hen (these are just slightly larger chickens that weigh about 2 pounds), or buy the smallest chicken you can find.

WHOLE POUSSIN

MAKES 2 SERVINGS

BRINE

1 GALLON WATER

1½ CUPS SUGAR

1 CUP KOSHER SALT

3 BAY LEAVES

1 HEAD GARLIC, HALVED HORIZONTALLY

1 MEDIUM ONION, THINLY SLICED

1 TABLESPOON BLACK PEPPERCORNS

2 LEMONS, HALVED

2 TABLESPOONS TARRAGON LEAVES

2 TABLESPOONS PARSLEY LEAVES

2 BLACK TEA BAGS

CHICKEN

2 WHOLE POUSSINS (ABOUT 1 POUND EACH), PREFERABLY WITH HEADS AND FEET INTACT (SEE RESOURCES, PAGE 108), BUTTERFLIED

EXTRA-VIRGIN OLIVE OIL, FOR DRIZZLING

FLAKY SEA SALT, SUCH AS MALDON

LEMON WEDGES, FOR SERVING

❶ In a stockpot, combine the water, sugar, salt, bay leaves, garlic, onion, and peppercorns. Squeeze the juice of the lemons into the pot and drop in the halves. Bring the mixture to a boil, stir to dissolve the sugar and salt, then turn off the heat. Add the tarragon, parsley, and tea bags and let steep for 20 minutes.

❷ Remove the tea bags and let the brine cool to room temperature, then transfer to a nonreactive container and refrigerate until chilled.

❸ Add the poussins to the brine and refrigerate for 3 to 4 hours.

❹ Set a wire rack over a rimmed baking sheet. Remove the poussins from the brine and rinse well; discard the brine. Pat the poussins dry with paper towels and place on the wire rack. Refrigerate for 6 hours.

❺ Prepare a two-stage fire with high and cool sides in a grill (see page 71).

❻ Place the poussins skin side down, on the hot side of the grill. Grill until dark grill marks

form, about 5 minutes. Move the poussins to the cool side of the grill, skin side up, cover the grill, and cook until an instant-read thermometer inserted into a leg registers 150°F, about 10 minutes.

2 Transfer the poussins to a platter, drizzle with olive oil, sprinkle with flaky salt, and serve with lemon wedges.

OIL EARLY AND OIL WELL

Before you put food on a hot grill, scrape off any leftover gunk with a wire brush. Then take a kitchen towel, roll it up into a tight cylinder, and tie it with twine. Grab a pair of tongs, dunk the towel into a bowl of vegetable oil, and rub down the grates. This first wipe-down cleans the grill. Wait a minute, then dunk the towel and wipe the grill again, and again a minute later, repeating the process until you've oiled the grill, about ten times if you're grilling a food that tends to stick, like fish or chicken. This repeated oiling may sound like OCD, but doing so really helps to create a nonstick seasoning on the grate that, like a cast-iron skillet, gets better and better over time. You don't have to be quite as fastidious if you're cooking something that won't stick—three or four rounds of wiping is sufficient for most other grilling tasks.

Also oil the food before it hits the grill. Coat all vegetables evenly with olive oil, which, in addition to helping the ingredients cook evenly, infuses the food with flavor as it cooks. However, don't oil red meat before grilling: That makes it harder to achieve that great charred crust. All but the leanest cuts of meat will start oozing fat the moment they hit the grill. If a steak, pork chop, or piece of chicken sticks to the grates when you try to turn it, you're flipping it too soon. Wait a minute, then try again; it'll release when it's ready.

GRILL-SMOKED CHICKEN WITH JAMAICAN GRAVY

This isn't a recipe for authentic jerk chicken by a long shot: instead of rubbing or marinating the chicken in the traditional seasoning—a lip-numbing blend of allspice, Scotch bonnet peppers, and other ingredients—you smoke the chicken over a mix of wood chips and jerk spices, then serve it with a tangy soy-based sauce infused with Scotch bonnets and allspice berries. The sauce is quite harsh just after it's made, but it will mellow as it ages, so make it at least a day ahead. If you live near a Jamaican market, you might be able to find some pimento wood sticks or chips (or see Resources, page 108); use them in place of the fruit wood for an even more jerk flavor.

THIGH

MAKES 4 SERVINGS

WOOD CHIP PACKET

¼ CUP WOOD CHIPS, PREFERABLY APPLE OR CHERRY WOOD, SOAKED IN WATER FOR AT LEAST 15 MINUTES AND DRAINED

3 TABLESPOONS ALLSPICE BERRIES

2 TABLESPOONS DRIED THYME

2 TABLESPOONS DRIED ROSEMARY

CHICKEN

8 BONE-IN, SKIN-ON CHICKEN THIGHS (ABOUT 3 POUNDS)

KOSHER SALT AND FRESHLY GROUND BLACK PEPPER

JAMAICAN GRAVY (RECIPE FOLLOWS)

❶ Prepare a two-stage fire with medium-high and low sides in a grill (see page 71) Oil the grate well.

❷ Place the wood chips in the middle of a 1-foot square of aluminum foil. Sprinkle the allspice berries, thyme, and rosemary over the chips and cover with a second piece of foil. Fold the sides over to make a flat packet about 6 inches square. Using a paring knife, poke holes all over the top of the packet. Place the foil packet on top of the coals in the medium-high side of the grill (or, if using a gas grill, lift the grate and place the foil directly on top of the burner).

❸ Season the chicken all over with salt and pepper. When the wood chip packet begins to smoke, place the chicken thighs, skin side down, on the grate over the packet. Grill the thighs, turning them every few minutes, until charred all over and cooked through (an instant-read thermometer inserted into the thickest part

of the meat should register 165°F), about 15 minutes. Transfer the chicken to a platter and let rest for a few minutes.

④ Drizzle the gravy over the chicken and serve, passing extra sauce on the side.

JAMAICAN GRAVY

Makes 4 cups

4 SCOTCH BONNET OR HABANERO PEPPERS

2 CUPS LOW-SODIUM SOY SAUCE

2 CUPS DISTILLED WHITE VINEGAR

3 TABLESPOONS ALLSPICE BERRIES

① Wearing a pair of latex gloves, cut the peppers into quarters, then remove the seeds and ribs.

② In a jar or an empty wine bottle, combine the soy sauce, vinegar, allspice, and peppers. Seal and shake a few times. Let stand for at least 1 day at room temperature (waiting a week is even better). The sauce's flavor will improve as it stands, and it can be stored at room temperature for several months.

ROOM-TEMPERATURE MEAT

You've probably read elsewhere that it's important to bring meat up to room temperature before smoking or grilling it, but I haven't found this to have any effect on the final product whatsoever. There's nothing wrong with letting meat warm up before cooking. In fact, I often take meat out of the refrigerator an hour or so before I cook it so I can apply a dry rub or, when grilling, salt the meat ahead of time. But taking meat directly from the fridge to the smoker is just fine; it will just take a little longer to cook.

DONENESS:
KNOW WHERE TO STICK IT

With barbecue, you cook to texture—that is, smoke the meat until it reaches the balance of tenderness and chewiness that you're looking for, which varies from cut to cut and animal to animal. But with grilled meats, you want to cook to temperature. It's the only way to ensure that the meat will be done to your liking. And how you like your meat grilled—just like how long you grow your hair or how milky you take your coffee—is your prerogative and yours only.

However you like it, cooking meat to the desired temperature is the hardest part of grilling, period. The difference between perfectly cooked and overdone can be a matter of moments, and any recipe's cooking time suggestions (including my own) are at best rough estimates—so many small and big factors can increase or decrease cooking time that the only way to know when it's done is to find out for yourself.

This, too, isn't as easy as it sounds. Many grilling enthusiasts swear by the "finger test" for determining doneness: you poke at a piece of meat, then poke the palm of your hand at the base of your thumb while pressing various fingers together to find the corresponding firmness. This is supposed to tell you when your meat is cooked to rare, medium-rare, and so on, but I've never understood the reasoning behind this hackneyed method. Different cuts and animals have different textures—a beef tenderloin cooked to medium might feel the same as a rare rib-eye, or a medium-rare pork chop the same as a desiccated chicken breast.

Other folks use the meat juices as an indicator of doneness. A chicken's juices are said to run clear when it's cooked through, but I've had undercooked chicken ooze clear juices and overcooked chicken run pink; this method is too inconsistent to be trusted. Some cooks will cut into the meat to take a peek inside to check its color. This is also misleading, as meat actually turns redder as it is exposed to oxygen, and different meats are naturally different shades of red—even within the same type of animal.

What *does* work to determine doneness is a good instant-read thermometer. It is accurate and consistent, as long as: (1) your thermometer can be trusted and (2) you know how to use it.

Concerning #1: As "scientific" instruments, most kitchen thermometers are as reliable as a career politician. Cheap thermometers can and will lie to you—or, at best, take too long to tell the truth. But if you find a digital instant-read thermometer that reads temperatures quickly and accurately, you'll never eat an overcooked steak again.

There are many cheaper instant-read options on the market and some of these even work well, but you should test any thermometer's accuracy first by dipping it into a pot of boiling water (it should register 212°F within a few seconds) and/or a bowl of ice water (32°F). Anything that takes longer than 5 seconds to display the correct temperature isn't an "instant-read" thermometer and won't serve you well at the grill. If the thermometer is quick but doesn't read the proper temperature, calibrate it (if this is an option) or try another model.

After you've found a thermometer you trust, learn how to use it: Always insert the thermometer into the thickest part of the meat, at least 1 inch away from any bones, which will be hotter than the meat around them. Repeat this in two or three spots near the center to confirm your first temperature reading. (Don't listen to folks who say that this will cause the meat to lose a lot of juices; meat is a sponge, not a balloon, and liquid loss will be minimal unless you treat the meat like a voodoo doll.) With steaks and chops, insert the thermometer through the side; this makes it easier to find the center of the cut. With whole chicken, insert the thermometer between the drumstick and the breast; with chicken breasts, insert the thermometer near the neck cavity into the thickest part of the breast. If you're not confident about the reading, test it again in a different part of the meat.

Keep in mind that meat will continue to cook after you've pulled it off the grill. Depending on the type and cut of meat, the internal temperature will generally rise by somewhere between 5 and 10 degrees as the meat rests, so remove it from the grill before it reaches the desired doneness.

THE IMPORTANCE OF RESTING

Resting grilled meat is essential; it lets the meat's muscle fibers relax, which allows its internal juices to be redistributed throughout the cut. Steaks, chops, and chicken parts need about 10 minutes of resting; a large roast or a whole chicken may need 20 minutes or longer. Some recipes tell you to tent resting meats with foil. I almost never do this: while covering meat with foil helps it (slightly) to stay warm, it also creates steam that will ruin the crispy crust or skin that you've worked so hard to obtain. It's better to let your meat rest uncovered, then rewarm it, if necessary, over a low-heat fire or in a warm oven.

GRILLING TEMPERATURES

The chart below gives my recommended cooking temperatures for various cuts of grilled meat. They are typically below USDA recommendations for "safely" cooked meat. As with many things in life, you have to balance safety with pleasure.

	DONENESS	INTERNAL TEMPERATURE (BEFORE RESTING)	USDA-RECOMMENDED INTERNAL TEMPERATURE
	Rare	115°F	
	Medium-Rare	125°F	145°F
BEEF	Medium	135°F	160°F
	Medium-Well	145°F	
	Well Done	155°F	170°F
	Ground Beef	160°F	160°F

	DONENESS	INTERNAL TEMPERATURE (BEFORE RESTING)	USDA-RECOMMENDED INTERNAL TEMPERATURE
PORK AND VEAL	Rare	120°F	
	Medium-Rare	130°F	145°F
	Medium	140°F	160°F
	Medium-Well	150°F	
	Well Done	160°F	170°F
	Ground Pork and Veal	160°F	160°F

	DONENESS	INTERNAL TEMPERATURE (BEFORE RESTING)	USDA-RECOMMENDED INTERNAL TEMPERATURE
LAMB	Rare	120°F	
	Medium-Rare	130°F	145°F
	Medium	140°F	160°F
	Medium-Well	145°F	
	Well Done	150°F	170°F
	Ground Lamb	160°F	170°F

	DONENESS	TEMPERATURE (OF THE THICKEST PART OF THE THIGH BEFORE RESTING)	USDA-RECOMMENDED INTERNAL TEMPERATURE
POULTRY	Cooked Through	165°F	165°F

CHICKEN SPIEDIES

Spiedies is essentially an Italian-Americanized kebab (the name comes from *spiedini*, the Italian word for skewered meat), made with various types of meat that is marinated and then grilled. This recipe calls for quotidian boneless, skinless chicken breasts, but you can make spiedies with any kind of tender skewer-friendly cut of pork, lamb, or beef. A soft roll—or, in some cases, white sandwich bread—is used to pull the grilled meat off the skewer, making for some of the best handheld food around.

BREAST

MAKES 6 SERVINGS

2 POUNDS BONELESS, SKINLESS CHICKEN BREASTS, CUT INTO 1-INCH CUBES

SPICY ITALIAN DRESSING (RECIPE FOLLOWS)

KOSHER SALT AND FRESHLY GROUND BLACK PEPPER

6 SOFT ITALIAN ROLLS, SPLIT

¼ CUP MELTED GARLIC BUTTER (PAGE 66) OR 4 TABLESPOONS UNSALTED BUTTER, MELTED

❶ Put the chicken in a large resealable plastic bag, add enough dressing to cover it, and seal the bag, pushing out any extra air. Refrigerate for at least 4 hours, or as long as overnight.

❷ Soak 6 long wooden skewers in water for 30 minutes (or use metal skewers). Prepare a medium-hot single-level fire in a grill (see page 71).

❸ Thread the chicken onto the skewers and season with salt and pepper. Discard the dressing. Grill the chicken, turning frequently (use tongs; you'll burn your fingers if you try to grab the skewers), until charred all over and cooked through, 8 to 10 minutes.

❹ Meanwhile, brush the cut side of the rolls with the melted butter and grill until toasted, 2 to 3 minutes.

❺ Place a skewer inside each roll and use the bread to hold the meat in place as you pull out the skewer. Drizzle with extra Italian dressing, if desired, and serve at once.

SPICY ITALIAN DRESSING

Makes about 1½ cups

½ CUP EXTRA-VIRGIN OLIVE OIL

½ CUP CANOLA OIL

¼ CUP DISTILLED WHITE VINEGAR

2 TABLESPOONS RED WINE VINEGAR

2 TEASPOONS DIJON MUSTARD

1 TEASPOON HONEY

1 GARLIC CLOVE, FINELY CHOPPED

1 MEDIUM SHALLOT, FINELY CHOPPED

3 TABLESPOONS FINELY CHOPPED PARSLEY

3 PEPPADEW PEPPERS, FINELY CHOPPED

1 TEASPOON KOSHER SALT

¼ TEASPOON DRIED OREGANO

PINCH OF RED PEPPER FLAKES

FRESHLY GROUND BLACK PEPPER

Combine all the ingredients in a jar with a lid, cover tightly, and shake well. The dressing can be refrigerated for up to 1 week.

ON THE
SIDE

My biggest barbecue inspiration has been the meat markets of central Texas. These barbecue joints began as butcher shops opened by German immigrants, who smoked brisket and sausages in outdoor pits and sold them by the pound. They weren't set up as restaurants with dedicated kitchens, so customers who wanted to eat on the premises would supplement their meals with whatever was being sold on the market's shelves—usually pickles, cheese, bread, and crackers. While I love the simplicity of this style of dining, I know that people do like to round out their meals with side dishes. When selecting appetizers or sides, pair barbecue with dishes that are high in acidity, which helps balance the richness of the meat. It's also smart to contrast hot barbecue with cold or room-temperature sides such as broccoli salad (see opposite) or coleslaw (see page 95), especially during hot summer months.

There's an obvious convenience that comes from cooking your sides on the grill. You can also use a smoker as an oven to bake beans, potatoes, or whatever will benefit from some time in the smoke chamber. When you've already got the heat (or smoke), why not use it?

CORA'S BROCCOLI SALAD

This salad is meant to be eaten at room temperature or cold, and its flavors actually improve after a day or two in the refrigerator, which gives the acidic vinaigrette enough time to soak into the crisp broccoli.

MAKES 4 SERVINGS

1 LARGE BUNCH BROCCOLI (ABOUT 1 POUND), CUT INTO 1-INCH FLORETS, WOODY STEMS DISCARDED

2 TABLESPOONS FRESH LEMON JUICE

1 LARGE GARLIC CLOVE, FINELY CHOPPED

PINCH OF RED PEPPER FLAKES

¼ CUP EXTRA-VIRGIN OLIVE OIL

KOSHER SALT AND FRESHLY GROUND BLACK PEPPER

① Place a steamer basket in a large saucepan, add 1 inch of water, and bring the water to a boil. Add the broccoli, cover, and steam until crisp-tender, about 5 minutes. Transfer the broccoli to a bowl and let cool.

② While the broccoli cools, make the vinaigrette: In a small bowl, whisk together the lemon juice, garlic, and red pepper flakes. Slowly whisk in the olive oil. Season with salt and pepper.

③ Toss the broccoli with the vinaigrette and serve immediately, or cover and refrigerate until ready to serve. The salad can be refrigerated for up to 2 days.

DANTE'S POTATO SALAD

This potato salad, while certainly in the German style, has an Italian flair in the form of olive oil. The addition of grainy mustard nudges it back toward Germany.

MAKES 8 TO 10 SERVINGS

½ CUP PLUS 1 TABLESPOON EXTRA-VIRGIN OLIVE OIL

1 LARGE SPANISH ONION, DICED

4 POUNDS YUKON GOLD OR OTHER WAXY POTATOES

KOSHER SALT

2 TABLESPOONS WHOLE-GRAIN MUSTARD

¼ CUP CIDER VINEGAR

¼ TEASPOON CAYENNE PEPPER

FRESHLY GROUND BLACK PEPPER

2 TABLESPOONS CHOPPED CHIVES

❶ In a large skillet, heat 1 tablespoon of the olive oil over medium-low heat. Add the onion and cook, stirring frequently, until translucent and crisp-tender (you don't want the onion to be completely soft), about 8 minutes; if the onion begins to brown, lower the heat. Transfer to a bowl and let cool.

❷ In a large saucepan, cover the potatoes with water by 1 inch and add a large pinch of salt. Bring the water to a boil, reduce the heat to a simmer, and cook until the potatoes are tender, about 25 minutes. Drain the potatoes and transfer to a cutting board.

❸ Meanwhile, in a bowl, whisk together the mustard, vinegar, and cayenne. Slowly whisk in the remaining ½ cup olive oil. Season the vinaigrette to taste with salt and black pepper.

❹ When the potatoes are cool enough to handle, cut into ½-inch dice.

❺ In a bowl, toss the warm potatoes and reserved onions with the vinaigrette. Add the chives, season with salt and black pepper, and toss again. The potato salad can be served immediately or refrigerated for up to 1 day.

SUSAN'S DILLY COLESLAW

This tangy slaw recipe is extremely simple—just mayonnaise, a touch of vinegar, and lots of dill—but you can treat it as a foundation and add other cabbages or vegetables as you see fit.

MAKES 8 SERVINGS

1 CUP MAYONNAISE

1 TABLESPOON DISTILLED WHITE VINEGAR

½ CUP CHOPPED DILL FRONDS

KOSHER SALT AND FRESHLY GROUND BLACK PEPPER

2 POUNDS WHITE OR NAPA CABBAGE (ABOUT ½ LARGE HEAD), CORED AND CUT INTO ¼-INCH-WIDE RIBBONS

❶ In a small bowl, whisk together the mayonnaise and vinegar. Stir in the dill and season the dressing to taste with salt and pepper.

❷ In a salad bowl, toss the cabbage with the dressing. Refrigerate for at least 1 hour before serving. The slaw can be refrigerated for up to 1 day.

BAKED BEANS WITH BURNT ENDS

Burnt ends are the trimmings left over from smoked brisket. Traditionally they were considered scraps not worthy of selling to customers, so they were given away or used in beans or stews. But barbecue lovers came to recognize burnt ends for what they are—densely flavored, intensely smoky nuggets of bark—and they became a delicacy. Add burnt ends to beans but also add any leftover scraps from carving pulled pork, barbecue belly, ribs, whatever. The more kinds of meat you add to the pot, the richer and more complex your beans will be. If you have especially fatty chunks of meat, stir them in earlier in the cooking process to allow the fat to melt and enrich the beans.

MAKES 8 SERVINGS

1 POUND GREAT NORTHERN BEANS, PICKED OVER

4 CUPS WATER

1 SMALL SPANISH ONION, THINLY SLICED

2 LARGE GARLIC CLOVES, FINELY CHOPPED

3 CUPS HEINZ KETCHUP

½ CUP BROWN ALE OR OTHER MALTY BEER

¼ CUP WORCESTERSHIRE SAUCE

½ CUP PACKED DARK BROWN SUGAR

2 TABLESPOONS COLMAN'S MUSTARD POWDER (SEE NOTE)

1 TABLESPOON KOSHER SALT

1 TABLESPOON FRESHLY GROUND BLACK PEPPER

½ TEASPOON CAYENNE PEPPER

1 BAY LEAF

1 POUND BRISKET BURNT ENDS OR ASSORTED BARBECUE, DICED (ABOUT 3 CUPS)

1 Put the beans in a medium bowl and cover with water by 2 inches. Soak for at least 8 hours at room temperature.

2 Preheat the oven to 250°F.

3 Drain the beans and put in a Dutch oven or other large pot. Add all remaining ingredients, except for any leaner pieces of meat, and bring to a boil. Cover the pot, transfer to the oven, and bake for 2 hours.

4 Uncover the pot and stir in any remaining meat. Return to the oven and bake for 2 hours longer. Remove the bay leaf and serve the beans. Or let cool and refrigerate for up to 2 days.

NOTE

There will be other brands of mustard powder on your grocery store shelf, but none will be nearly as intense as Colman's. If you use the weak stuff, you'll be disappointed.

COLLARD GREENS

Collard greens are excellent with smoked meat. The liquid left from cooking the greens into submission is what's known as pot liquor (or "potlikker"), a vinegary, porky broth that's magical in and of itself. Save any leftover potlikker to use in soups or gravies—some Southerners even drink it straight as a tonic.

MAKES 4 TO 6 SERVINGS

2 LARGE BUNCHES COLLARD GREENS (ABOUT 3 POUNDS)

4 SLICES THICK-CUT BACON, CUT INTO 1-INCH PIECES

2 GARLIC CLOVES, FINELY CHOPPED

1 SMOKED HAM HOCK, RINSED

8 CUPS WATER

ONE 12-OUNCE BOTTLE PILSNER BEER

¼ CUP CIDER VINEGAR, OR MORE TO TASTE

2 TABLESPOONS DARK BROWN SUGAR

1 BAY LEAF

SMALL PINCH RED PEPPER FLAKES

¼ TEASPOON YELLOW MUSTARD SEEDS

1 TABLESPOON KOSHER SALT, OR MORE TO TASTE

1 TEASPOON FRESHLY GROUND BLACK PEPPER

① Cut or tear the woody stems and ribs from the collard greens, and discard any leaves that are bruised or yellow. Wash and drain the leaves (you don't have to dry them well). Stack a few leaves at a time and roll them up like a cigar, then cut crosswise into ½-inch-wide strips.

② In a stockpot, cook the bacon over medium-low heat until some of the fat has rendered, about 8 minutes. Add the garlic and cook, stirring, for 2 minutes.

③ Add the ham hock, water, beer, cider vinegar, brown sugar, bay leaf, red pepper flakes, mustard seeds, salt, and pepper to the pot, then add the collard greens, packing them down until they're submerged in the liquid. Bring the liquid to a boil, then lower the heat to a simmer, cover the pot, leaving a crack for steam to escape, and cook, stirring occasionally, until the collards are very tender, at least 2 hours.

④ Remove and discard the bay leaf (if you can find it). Remove the ham hock from the greens and, when it is cool enough to handle, remove the skin and pull the meat from the bone. Coarsely chop the meat and return it to the pot.

⑤ Season the greens with more salt and/or vinegar, if necessary. Serve, or let cool and refrigerate for up to 1 day.

CHARRED BROCCOLI WITH PECORINO AND LEMON

Vegetables cooked in a blazing-hot skillet until they are almost blackened take on a meaty, deeply caramelized flavor. This can also be done on the grill. Make sure to coat the broccoli all over with oil; this will help distribute heat for even charring. You can also make the recipe with smaller broccoli florets in a grill basket.

MAKES 4 SERVINGS

1 LARGE HEAD BROCCOLI
(ABOUT 1 POUND)

3 TABLESPOONS EXTRA-VIRGIN OLIVE
OIL, PLUS MORE FOR DRIZZLING

KOSHER SALT

¼ CUP FINELY GRATED PECORINO-
ROMANO CHEESE

FINELY GRATED ZEST OF 1 LEMON

FLAKY SEA SALT, SUCH AS MALDON

1 Prepare a medium-hot single-level fire in a grill (see page 71).

2 Trim about 2 inches off the end of the broccoli stalk and cut the broccoli into 8 long spears. In a bowl, toss the broccoli with the olive oil until well coated, then season lightly with kosher salt.

3 Grill the broccoli spears, turning them every couple of minutes, until charred all over and crisp-tender, about 8 minutes.

4 Transfer the broccoli to a platter and drizzle with olive oil. Sprinkle with the cheese, lemon zest, and flaky salt and serve immediately.

CHARRED LONG BEANS

A speckling of blistered flesh on vegetables adds both caramelized and smoky flavors, which are so much more interesting than anything a steamer can achieve. Chinese long beans are especially grill-friendly, as their length and curly shape will prevent them from slipping through the grates. They make an easy, extra-quick side dish that you can cook in the time it takes for meat to rest after it comes off the grill.

MAKES 4 SERVINGS

1 POUND CHINESE LONG BEANS, TRIMMED

2 TABLESPOONS EXTRA-VIRGIN OLIVE OIL

KOSHER SALT AND FRESHLY GROUND BLACK PEPPER

3 TABLESPOONS MELTED GARLIC BUTTER (PAGE 66)

¼ CUP CHOPPED PARSLEY

① Prepare a medium-hot single-level fire in a grill (see page 71).

② Bring a large pot of salted water to a boil. Prepare an ice bath. Blanch the beans for 1 minute, then transfer to the ice bath. When they are cool, drain the beans.

③ Put the beans on a rimmed baking sheet, drizzle with the olive oil, and toss until coated, then season with salt and pepper.

④ Grill the beans, moving and turning them frequently with tongs, until crisp-tender and charred in spots, about 3 minutes.

⑤ Transfer the beans to a serving bowl and drizzle with the warm garlic butter. Sprinkle with the parsley and season with salt and pepper. Toss and serve.

CHARRED CORN WITH COMPOUND CREAM CHEESE

There are plenty of grilled corn recipes that call for a compound butter that's spread over the warm corn. Using a compound cream cheese is a similar concept, but the cheese adds a bit of tang, and it sticks to the ears better than butter. The cream cheese is flavored with za'atar, a Middle Eastern spice blend made from sesame seeds, sumac, and other spices and dried herbs. It's nutty and herby, with a distinct tartness from the sumac.

MAKES 8 SERVINGS

4 OUNCES CREAM CHEESE, AT ROOM TEMPERATURE

1 TABLESPOON ZA'ATAR
(SEE RESOURCES, PAGE 108),
PLUS MORE FOR SPRINKLING

½ TEASPOON FINELY GRATED LEMON ZEST

1 TABLESPOON FRESH LEMON JUICE

KOSHER SALT AND FRESHLY GROUND BLACK PEPPER

8 EARS CORN, SHUCKED

OLIVE OIL, FOR BRUSHING

① Prepare a hot single-level fire in a grill (see page 71).

② In a small bowl, combine the cream cheese, za'atar, lemon zest, and lemon juice and mix with a fork until smooth. Season to taste with salt and pepper.

③ Brush the corn all over with olive oil and grill, turning every minute or so, until blistered and charred all over, 8 to 10 minutes.

④ Transfer the corn to a platter and use a butter knife to spread the cream cheese all over it. Sprinkle with za'atar and serve.

GRILLED CAULIFLOWER

Any cruciferous vegetable tastes better with some char on it. Here, cauliflower's natural sweetness is boosted by dousing it in a quick salty-sweet marinade. This technique works equally well with broccoli, but be sure to cook either vegetable until just crisp-tender, with a little bit of bite.

MAKES 4 APPETIZER OR SIDE-DISH SERVINGS

3 TABLESPOONS TAMARI

3 TABLESPOONS BALSAMIC VINEGAR

1 TABLESPOON EXTRA-VIRGIN OLIVE OIL, PLUS MORE FOR DRIZZLING

1 HEAD CAULIFLOWER (ABOUT 2 POUNDS), CORED AND CUT INTO 1-INCH FLORETS

KOSHER SALT

1 TABLESPOON FINELY CHOPPED PARSLEY

FLAKY SEA SALT, SUCH AS MALDON

1 Prepare a hot single-level fire in a grill (see page 71).

2 In a large bowl, whisk together the tamari and vinegar. Slowly whisk in the olive oil. Add the cauliflower and toss until well coated. Season lightly with kosher salt.

3 Place a grill basket on the grill and add the cauliflower. (If your grill basket isn't large enough to hold the cauliflower in a single layer, cook it in two batches.) Grill the cauliflower, tossing frequently, until crisp-tender and caramelized all over, 10 to 12 minutes.

4 Transfer the cauliflower to a platter. Drizzle with olive oil, sprinkle with the parsley and flaky salt, and serve.

GRILLED SHISHITO PEPPERS

It's hard to beat the earthy, smoky scent of bell peppers being roasted over an open stovetop flame. When grilled, shishito peppers—the Japanese cousin of the Spanish Padrón pepper—acquire that same lovely flavor, though eating them can be a game of chance: most shishitos are mild, but about one in ten will smack you in the mouth with a spicy surprise.

MAKES 4 APPETIZER SERVINGS

20 SHISHITO PEPPERS

2 TABLESPOONS OLIVE OIL

KOSHER SALT AND FRESHLY GROUND BLACK PEPPER

FLAKY SEA SALT, SUCH AS MALDON

LIME WEDGES, FOR SERVING

1 Prepare a hot single-level fire in a grill (see page 71).

2 In a bowl, toss the peppers with the olive oil until well coated. Season with kosher salt and pepper.

3 Place a grill basket on the grill and add the peppers. Grill, tossing frequently, until blistered all over and charred in a few spots, 2 to 3 minutes.

4 Transfer the peppers to a platter and sprinkle with flaky salt. Serve with lime wedges.

GRILLED FINGERLING POTATOES

This simple side dish can be served alongside any meat or other main course you're throwing on the grill. A hot grill crisps up the exterior of the fingerlings so they are like fat steak fries, making them the perfect starch accompaniment.

MAKES 4 SERVINGS

1 POUND FINGERLING POTATOES, SCRUBBED

KOSHER SALT

EXTRA-VIRGIN OLIVE OIL

FRESHLY GROUND BLACK PEPPER

¼ CUP MELTED GARLIC BUTTER (PAGE 66)

¼ CUP CHOPPED PARSLEY

❶ Put the potatoes in a large saucepan and add enough water to cover by 2 inches. Add 1 tablespoon salt and bring to a boil over high heat. Reduce the heat to medium and simmer until the potatoes are just tender, about 10 minutes. Drain and let cool slightly, then cut lengthwise in half.

❷ Prepare a hot single-level fire in a grill (see page 71).

❸ In a large bowl, toss the potatoes with olive oil until well coated. Season with salt and pepper and toss again. Grill the potatoes, cut side down, until charred on the first side, 2 to 3 minutes. Turn the potatoes over and grill until the skin is crispy, about 2 minutes longer.

❹ Transfer the potatoes to a bowl and toss with the garlic butter. Season with salt and pepper, sprinkle with the parsley, and toss again. Transfer to a serving bowl and serve.

RESOURCES

TOOLS, ACCESSORIES, AND INGREDIENTS

Grilling and Barbecue Tools

SUR LA TABLE
surlatable.com
Grilling tools and accessories

THERMOWORKS
thermoworks.com
Instant-read thermometers and digital timers

WILLIAMS SONOMA
williams-sonoma.com
Grilling gear and grill baskets

Charcoal and Wood

B&B CHARCOAL
bbcharcoal.com
Lump charcoal and wood

PIMENTO WOOD
pimentowood.com
Pimento chips, sticks, and charcoal

THE WOODMAN LLC
thewoodman.com
Cooking wood and accessories

Grills and Smokers

BRINKMANN
brinkmann.net
Grills and smokers

CAMERONS
cameronsproducts.com
Stovetop smokers

GRILLWORKS
grillery.com
Argentinean-style wood grills

HOME DEPOT
homedepot.com
Grills, smokers, accessories, and fuel

SPITJACK
spitjack.com
Tuscan grills and rotisseries

WEBER
weber.com
Grills, smokers, and accessories

Ingredients

BO BO POULTRY
bobochicken.com
Rare-breed chickens, guinea hens, and poussins

FOSSIL FARMS
fossilfarms.com
Exotic meats and game

HERITAGE FOODS USA
heritagefoodsusa.com
Heritage-breed pork, beef, lamb, goat, and poultry

MURRAY'S CHEESE
murrayscheese.com
Halloumi, burrata, and other specialty cheeses

PENZEYS SPICES
penzeys.com
Spices and salts, including curing salt

RANCHO GORDO
ranchogordo.com
Pinquito and other heirloom beans

CONVERSION CHARTS

Here are rounded-off equivalents between the metric system and the traditional systems that are used in the United States to measure weight and volume.

FRACTIONS	DECIMALS
1/8	.125
1/4	.25
1/3	.33
3/8	.375
1/2	.5
5/8	.625
2/3	.67
3/4	.75
7/8	.875

WEIGHTS

US/UK	METRIC
1/4 oz	7 g
1/2 oz	15 g
1 oz	30 g
2 oz	55 g
3 oz	85 g
4 oz	110 g
5 oz	140 g
6 oz	170 g
7 oz	200 g
8 oz (1/2 lb)	225 g
9 oz	250 g
10 oz	280 g
11 oz	310 g
12 oz	340 g
13 oz	370 g
14 oz	400 g
15 oz	425 g
16 oz (1 lb)	455 g

VOLUME

AMERICAN	IMPERIAL	METRIC
1/4 tsp		1.25 ml
1/2 tsp		2.5 ml
1 tsp		5 ml
1/2 Tbsp (1 1/2 tsp)		7.5 ml
1 Tbsp (3 tsp)		15 ml
1/4 cup (4 Tbsp)	2 fl oz	60 ml
1/3 cup (5 Tbsp)	2 1/2 fl oz	75 ml
1/2 cup (8 Tbsp)	4 fl oz	125 ml
2/3 cup (10 Tbsp)	5 fl oz	150 ml
3/4 cup (12 Tbsp)	6 fl oz	175 ml
1 cup (16 Tbsp)	8 fl oz	250 ml
1 1/4 cups	10 fl oz	300 ml
1 1/2 cups	12 fl oz	350 ml
2 cups (1 pint)	16 fl oz	500 ml
2 1/2 cups	20 fl oz (1 pint)	625 ml
5 cups	40 fl oz (1 qt)	1.25 l

OVEN TEMPERATURES

	°F	°C	GAS MARK
very cool	250–275	130–140	1/2–1
cool	300	148	2
warm	325	163	3
moderate	350	177	4
moderately hot	375–400	190–204	5–6
hot	425	218	7
very hot	450–475	232–245	8–9

°C/F TO °F/C CONVERSION CHART

°C/F	°C	°F	°C/F	°C	°F	°C/F	°C	°F	°C/F	°C	°F
90	32	194	220	104	428	350	177	662	480	249	896
100	38	212	230	110	446	360	182	680	490	254	914
110	43	230	240	116	464	370	188	698	500	260	932
120	49	248	250	121	482	380	193	716	510	266	950
130	54	266	260	127	500	390	199	734	520	271	968
140	60	284	270	132	518	400	204	752	530	277	986
150	66	302	280	138	536	410	210	770	540	282	1,004
160	71	320	290	143	554	420	216	788	550	288	1,022
170	77	338	300	149	572	430	221	806			
180	82	356	310	154	590	440	227	824			
190	88	374	320	160	608	450	232	842			
200	93	392	330	166	626	460	238	860			
210	99	410	340	171	644	470	243	878			

Example: If your temperature is 90°F, your conversion is 32°C; if your temperature is 90°C, your conversion is 194°F.

INDEX

Library of Congress Cataloging-in-Publication Data

Names: Carroll, Joe, 1970- author. | Fauchald, Nick, author.
Title: Barbecue rules : lessons and recipes for superior smoking and grilling / Joe Carroll and Nick Fauchald ; photographs by William Hereford.
Description: New York : Artisan, a division of Workman Publishing Co.,Inc. [2019]. | Series: The Artisanal kitchen | Includes index.
Identifiers: LCCN 2018039181 | ISBN 9781579658687 (hardcover : alk. paper)
Subjects: LCSH: Barbecuing. | Smoked meat. | Barbecue sauce. | LCGFT: Cookbooks.
Classification: LCC TX840.B3 C3368 2019 | DDC 641.7/6--dc23
LC record available at https://lccn.loc.gov/2018039181

Cover and book design adapted by Hanh Le from *Feeding the Fire*, designed by Toni Tajima

Artisan books are available at special discounts when purchased in bulk for premiums and sales promotions as well as for fund-raising or educational use. Special editions or book excerpts also can be created to specification. For details, contact the Special Sales Director at the address below, or send an e-mail to specialmarkets@workman.com.

For speaking engagements, contact speakersbureau@workman.com.

Published by Artisan
A division of Workman Publishing Co., Inc.
225 Varick Street
New York, NY 10014-4381
artisanbooks.com

Artisan is a registered trademark of Workman Publishing Co., Inc.

This book has been adapted from *Feeding the Fire* (Artisan, 2015).

Published simultaneously in Canada by Thomas Allen & Son, Limited

Printed in China
First printing, January 2019

10 9 8 7 6 5 4 3 2 1